D1527689

Enabling Openness:
The future of the information society in Latin America and the Caribbean

Edited by
Bruce Girard and Fernando Perini

Fundación Comunica
Montevideo, Uruguay

International Development Research Centre
Ottawa • Cairo • Montevideo • Nairobi • New Delhi

Enabling Openness: The future of the information society in Latin
America and the Caribbean

Edited by: Bruce Girard and Fernando Perini

Fundación Comunica
Pablo de María 1036
Montevideo 11200
Uruguay
www.comunica.org / info@comunica.org

A copublication with:

International Development Research Centre
PO Box 8500
Ottawa, ON K1G 3H9
Canada
www.idrc.ca / info@idrc.ca

Diseño gráfico: Rodolfo Fuentes/NAO

ISBN 978-1-55250-578-6 (print)
ISBN 978-1-55250-579-3 (e-book)

Enabling Openness:
The future of the information society in Latin America and the Caribbean

Edited by
Bruce Girard and Fernando Perini

Comunica

IDRC | CRDI   Canadä

CONTENTS

Section 3: Digital citizenship: From representative to interactive democracy

Section 4: Copyright laws and the creative economy

Section 5: Privacy

PROLOGUE

Internet, openness and the future of the information society in LAC

Fernando Perini[1]

Over the past ten years, the internet has emerged as a central issue for development in Latin America and the Caribbean. The internet and other network technologies have shown their potential to increase productivity and competitiveness in the economy, to create new ways to deliver education and health services, and to be driving forces for the modernisation of the provision of public services. Despite the many challenges that the region still faces, the initially disparate use of the internet in education, governance, health and the productive sector has increasingly permeated national public policy and ongoing regional dialogues. As shown in the increased investments in broadband infrastructure in the region, there is a growing consensus that human development and economic growth rely largely on adequate access to and effective use of new information and communications technologies.

At the same time, the regional agenda is also reaching a tipping point. There is little doubt that the internet will continue to catalyse significant changes in Latin America and the Caribbean. However, as digital technologies affect new dimensions of economic, social and political life in the region, the debate about the potential of the internet for development is also more diverse (and dispersed). As we think about the future of the information society in the region, there are many

---

1   Senior Programme Officer at the International Development Research Centre.

1

unanswered questions about the internet and its contribution to development.

- Will the internet in Latin America and the Caribbean remain open over the next ten years?
- Will online surveillance increasingly challenge individual privacy?
- Will open data, social media and new forms of participation improve democracy in the region?
- Will we be able to harness the collaborative potential of the internet to create more socially meaningful and sustainable economies?
- Will digital education, science and creativity flourish in the region, reflecting the diversity and culture of its people?

These questions highlight some of the emerging issues that will be central to determining whether or not the internet will effectively contribute to a more open and developed society in our corner of the world.

Despite the many unknowns, one thing is clear: decisions we take now will determine how "open" or "closed" our societies will be in the future. Many countries in the region are reforming legislation and institutions to adapt to the digital age, and issues such as copyright, net neutrality, data protection, access to information and freedom of expression have an increasingly central position on their political agendas. However, we have seen that changes in the region have not necessarily been easy or positive.

This book includes a number of reflections and perspectives addressing the opportunities and challenges in relation to these emerging policy challenges, building on the seminar Open Development: Exploring the future of the information society in Latin America and the Caribbean 2000-2025 held in Montevideo on 2-3 April 2013. As government officials and experts gathered in Montevideo for the Fourth Ministerial Conference on the Information Society in Latin America and the Caribbean to review and discuss the regional agenda, the International Development Research Centre worked together with Fundación Comunica to organise the seminar as a pre-event. Building on a research agenda that sought to explore the emerging set of possibilities to catalyse positive change through "open" information-networked activities in international development,[2] we promoted this space to reflect on the direction of the changes happening in the region, bringing new themes to the table and exploring how they can better be addressed in regional efforts.

This book contains 25 short chapters organised into six sections dealing with the themes of the seminar. In order to create a rich and informed debate, we partnered with a number of leading organisations in Latin America and the Caribbean to identify key issues and explore different views and perspectives. We are very thankful to our thematic coordinators, Hernán Galperin from DIRSI, Sandro Jiménez-Ocampo from KolaborAccion, Geoff Schwarten from NESsT, Ronaldo Lemos and Joana Varon from Fundaçao Getulio Vargas and Claudio Ruiz from Derechos Digitales, as well as our many contributors who made this collective reflection possible. Also, Valeria Betancourt from APC and Manuel Acevedo enriched the discussion by connecting it with a review of our past experiences in regional collaboration. The partnership with AGESIC, the Uruguayan agency responsible for e-government, and UN-ECLAC was key for developing synergies between the open consultation and the participants attending the ministerial meeting. Finally, we need to acknowledge the fundamental contribution of Prof. Robin Mansell, who was supportive of this initiative from the beginning. Her contributions were essential

---

2   Smith, Matthew L., Laurent Elder, and Heloise Emdon. 2011. "Open Development: A new theory for ICT4D." *Information Technologies & International Development 7.1* (2011): pp-iii.

to contextualise this regional conversation within the global debate about openness in the information society. This book is being simultaneously published in English and Spanish thanks to the translation and copyediting team of Lori Nordstrom, Clio Bugel and Guillermo Vicens. Special thanks to Estela Acosta y Lara for her tireless and meticulous coordination of translation, copyediting and overall production of the volume.

The conversation also extended beyond the physical limitations of the seminar and the resulting chapters reflect an online and offline engagement with a wide and active community of academics, policy-makers and activists. The public conversations that led to this publication started a few months before the event in Montevideo, when the expert panel coordinators published blog posts on the questions highlighted above. Their contributions started an online conversation and provided a basis for the reflections of the panellists and participants in the seminar. Rather than traditional presentations, the interventions from panellists and participants revolved around these key questions. Thus, there were many opportunities for interaction among experts in the plenary sessions and smaller groups. In addition, the website "25 Years of the Information Society in LAC 2000-2025"[3] bridged online and offline conversations, providing a platform that archives the interactions and debates, including videos of the discussions. This process enriched the contributions and established dialogues that are —at least partially— reflected in this publication.

This book does not seek to present a consolidated perspective or unified vision. It is a collection of informed reflections and perspectives on new opportunities and challenges for the information society in the region and despite many points of agreement, there is also a considerable amount of diversity in the way authors frame the problems and seek new solutions. We

---

3   www.info25.org

believe that this diversity of informed perspectives is welcome as it contributes to the richness of the discussion and reflects the interest of engaging multiple actors in the debate. Moreover, this book is not meant to provide an exhaustive account of the evidence in relation to the different themes. Each one of the topics is complex and worthy of extended analysis and debate. Indeed, many of the people contributing to this publication are involved in the development of high-quality evidence in specific theme areas. Here, the objective was to reach a balance between insightful analysis which can inform the debate on specific issues and wider dialogue bringing together topics that are usually considered in isolation. We believe that a conversation about the future of the information society cannot ignore the linkages among these different topics. Therefore, establishing bridges among those involved in different themes is particularly useful when thinking about the future of our information society.

We hope that the depth and diversity of the contributions in this book and the connections among them reflect our increasingly networked society. Together, they show that while there are important forces driving change in specific directions, there is a common belief that we are all agents in building the future of the information society. Different pathways for development remain open. The quality of the dialogue reflected here shows that we are developing the basis for making informed decisions about these new themes and there are many opportunities for working together to make sure that we actively shape the pathway that we will follow and effectively build more inclusive and prosperous information societies in Latin America and the Caribbean.

INTRODUCTION

Imagining the Internet:
Open, closed or in between?

Robin Mansell[1]

The policies and practices aimed at facilitating inclusive information societies in the Latin American and Caribbean region, as in all regions of the world, are underpinned by the assumptions people make about how change happens. In the present era nearly all stakeholders are aware of changes in society that are accompanying rapid innovation and investment in digital information and communication technologies. This awareness may stem from their active use of digital applications and services or it may be the result of their exclusion from closed networks and services or even from those that are open for reasons of lack of access, financial resources or skills. Many cultural, social, political and economic factors influence the particular ways in which stakeholders envisage how change in information societies happens, how best to shape these changes towards desirable goals, and the consequences of different pathways in particular locales, countries and regions. These visions and assumptions about the future of information societies are underpinned by deeply embedded imaginaries which inform the decisions of all the stakeholders involved in these changes.

1   Robin Mansell is Chair of the Scientific Committee of the annual European Communications Policy Research Conference; a member of the Promotions Board at Institute of Development Studies (IDS), Sussex, where she was a trustee, 1999-2009. She is a member of Scientific Advisory Council, LIRNEAsia, Sri Lanka. She was President of the International Association for Media and Communication Research (IAMCR), 2004-2008 and remains and active member of IAMCR's Scholarly Review Committee and Finance Committee.

Social imaginaries can be understood as the way people imagine their social existence or as the Canadian philosopher, Charles Taylor put it, "how they fit together with others, how things go on between them and their fellows, the expectations which are normally met, and the deeper normative notions and images which underlie these expectations".[2] How do today's social imaginaries inform the way stakeholders think about the present and future of information societies and the consequences for development? Very simply, there are two prevailing social imaginaries about digital technologies, the Internet, mobile phones and their applications, both of which involve a deep commitment to the idea that these technologies provide opportunities for building 'good' or just and equitable societies. The prevailing dominant imaginary in today's information societies is market-led. In contrast, alternative imaginaries are best described as 'open' or commons-led. Progress towards the realization of one of these imaginaries is typically seen as being damaging to the realization of the other. It is this conflict that leads to major problems for stakeholders in deciding which policies and strategies, or mix of policies and strategies, is most likely to facilitate progress towards more just and equitable information societies.

The dominant imaginary is one of a universal 'information society' in which digital technologies and their applications are directly associated with 'digital enlightenment' or knowledge which can be applied with relatively little investment, apart from that required to achieve connectivity and access to digital information. It assumes that competition among technology and service suppliers is the best way to achieve widespread access to information (and knowledge) and that state security is a very high priority even if this involves surveillance, privacy intrusions and secrecy. Commercial expansion is assumed to be the optimal pathway towards inclusive participation in the information society, achieved through the increasing personalization of

---

2   Taylor, Charles. 2007. *A Secular Age*. Cambridge MA: Belknap Press.

digital services and the extension and enforcement of existing copyright legislation to create incentives for the production and consumption of digital products and services.

The 'open' or commons-led alternative imaginaries are characterized by some form of 'digital resistance' to the universal model of the information society. This usually involves some from of countervailing power, a privileging of co-operation and collaboration over competition, and innovative forms of networked collaboration often by dispersed communities. These imaginaries assume that trusting relationships can be fostered in information societies by maximizing information and decision making transparency through open access to information and by encouraging information sharing, facilitated by new approaches to information ownership.

The dominant imaginary of the information society gives a priority to technological innovation, often focusing on the benefits of technological convergence and opportunities created by the increasing modularity, miniaturization, and interoperability of digital services based on multiple platforms and intense market competition. In this imaginary, the principle focus, for example, is often on the diffusion of mobile phones or smart phones and on connectivity and access to information.

Policy often focuses principally on the spread of access to broadband networks and on the growth of commercial markets for digital content creation and aggregation. Debates tend to be concentrated on the rate of investment in network infrastructures and the implications of leadership in this area for the development of web browsing, peer-2-peer, Voice over Internet Protocol (VoIP), apps and user contributed video, but in terms of Internet traffic growth and revenues. The public policy debate focuses much less on developments in the 'private' or closed Internet for the managed digital services which increasingly supports digital television, Internet Protocol television (IPTV) and Internet Protocol telephony, nearly all of which are led by the commercial market strategies of private companies. These developments have major implications for the way citizens will experience their information societies in the future and whether they are able to access digital services that are open and available for collaborative sharing or closed and restricted to those who are able to participate in the market. This has implications for whether future digital environments are consistent with the values of freedom of expression and inclusive citizen participation which are aligned with the alternative imaginaries of information societies.

In the dominant imaginary of the information society, information is deemed to have economic value and the policy priority is to ensure that intellectual property rights legislation is designed and enforced to enable the exploitation of this value. In contrast, in the alternative imaginaries, digital information is assumed to 'want to be free'. There are differences among stakeholders who align with this view, but the main priority for policy is to maximize opportunities for open access to information. Conflicts arise between those seeking to enforce copyright protections and social movements that seek to set information 'free', for example, through copyright infringing file sharing of music and other digital content or through collaborative online contributions that are open for use and reuse by all.

In the dominant social imaginary of the information society with its emphasis on technological innovation, a key priority is to promote the increasing sophistication of the automated collection and processing of digital information. Automation is giving rise to new potentials for the surveillance of all online activities by both the State and the private sector. Increasingly, citizens can 'click' but they cannot 'hide'. In alternative imaginaries, these developments are seen as having substantial implications for human rights and for whether or not future information societies are consistent with the values of transparency and democratic participation in society.

Proponents of alternative imaginaries of information societies are well aware that digital platforms can be used for malicious attacks against both individuals and the State. In some cases, States are using digital network capabilities to respond with force and companies are using these automated surveillance capabilities to develop sophisticated targeted advertising and marketing techniques. These automation techniques for information processing are also giving rise to major new initiatives to take advantage of vast repositories of digital information or 'big data' for an increasing variety of mapping and visualization applications, many with beneficial development implications in fields such as health and the environment. However, here too there are contests between the dominant and alternative imaginaries of information societies. In the former, 'big data' may be closed and exclusive to its owners; in the latter, such data are seen as a public resource that can be mined and applied when it is managed in an open way.

The dominant and alternative imaginaries of information societies are deeply contested. The specific form of contestation is expressed in different ways in various regions of the world depending on their histories, cultural contexts, social, economic and political characteristics, and institutional environments. In the case of each of the key issue areas discussed so far, the central question that needs to be asked is who is benefiting from information societies now and who will benefit in the future? Are those benefits fairly and equitably distributed? If they are not, what measures should be taken by the State, companies, and other actors, including NGOs and citizens, to redress imbalances where they persist?

These imaginaries of information societies matter because the present bias is toward the dominant model favouring market-led developments and focusing on information exchange, information scarcity secured through copyright, and rapid technological innovation and mastery. This contrasts with alternative models which favour a widening of the information commons to foster information sharing, information abundance, and generative innovation from the bottom up. The challenge for policy and practice is how to achieve a better balance between these contending approaches.

The contests between the two models will persist and continue to challenge policy makers and practitioners for two major reasons. These are related to two key paradoxes which are present in all of today's information societies regardless of their position in the rankings for broadband, Internet and mobile penetration or access to information.

The first is the 'paradox of information': information is costly to produce and intellectual property rights create incentives for creativity, diversity and growth; and, information is virtually costless to reproduce and incentives are created for creativity, diversity and growth when it is feely distributed. The second is the 'paradox of complexity': the intrinsic benefits of complexity (mainly non-transparent automation of information processing) in the digital system are leading to decreasing control through traditional means of governance; and, the intrinsic benefits of complexity in the digital system are leading to enhanced control and new modes of governance within a decentralized network system.

The result of these paradoxes is that there are frictions and resistance among oppositional groups whose principal interests lie mainly with one or the other features of these paradoxes. With respect to the information paradox, there are many new ways to legitimize the open circulation of information and so contestations in this area, though likely to persist, may become less trenchant as policy makers and the private sector introduce new hybrid approaches that balance interests in open and closed information environments. In the case of the second paradox, however, strong advocacy for market-led development of information societies without regulation because of the perceived risks of intervening in a complex technological system with uncertain outcomes is likely to persist. It will be accompanied by strong advocacy for policy that promotes transparency and accountability of State and private companies in order to ensure that human rights to privacy are protected and expectations for citizen safety and security are met.

Regardless of which imaginary of information societies is privileged, measures that accommodate conflicting interests are unlikely to be effective when the main focus of policy is on technology, e.g. ICT hardware, software, networks and services, instead of on human relationships within information societies. Technologies are not proxies for the knowledge people draw upon in order to make sense of their world. They are not proxies for 'how things go on between them and their fellows'. In the face of paradoxes such that infuse information societies with contradictions and conflict among stakeholders, the best way forward is to consider the interlinked policy corrections that are needed to counter monopolies of knowledge wherever they appear.

For example, the claim that there is a universal information society is one such monopolistic argument. Countering this 'imaginary' means addressing how best to foster multiple approaches within and outside the commercial marketplace. It requires initiatives to roll back expansionist intellectual property legislation, giving attention to the specific needs, resources and strengths of particular markets and collaborative cultures in the different countries and regions. It also requires deliberation on the appropriate limits of intrusive online surveillance and privacy invasions, consistent with human rights and freedom of expression and acknowledging that the complexity of today's digital networks and applications means that the surveillance (State and corporate) which is possible today may become more excessive in the future, if it is not governed effectively.

Policy corrections are needed to effectively institutionalize procedures for holding states and companies accountable through legislation, policy and regulation, and for holding dispersed online communities accountable as well. In practice, this means that policy for information societies needs to shift from the present situation in which the majority of interventions are top down and strongly driven by technological innovation, towards policy that gives greater emphasis to bottom–up accountable interventions that are responsive to local circumstances. To take just one example, the enthusiasm for 'big data' and crowdsourcing is being driven by top down policy in the name of acquiring new information resources that are scientifically validated and curated, consistent with the dominant imaginary which seeks to maintain, preserve and add value to digital research data throughout its life cycle, the goal being the accumulation of knowledge for formal science and technological innovation. In contrast, there are increasing examples of 'big data' leading to knowledge that is useful for local actors which rely on voluntary contributions of distributed groups using open methods for validated information that can be applied in social problem solving. This alternative is supported by an imaginary which values informal norms for openly sharing information with the goal of generating useful knowledge for immediate application to social problems.

In conclusion, in the light of the paradoxes of information and complexity in today's information societies, a key issue is whether the future is likely to bring continuing and deeper conflicts among stakeholders with different interests or whether there is potential for temporary reconciliation of the goals of market-led economic growth and open development in future information societies. The hope for reconciliation rests on the capacity of all stakeholders to reject the hegemonic universal vision of *the* information society while also resisting reactionary forms of bottom-up localism that ignore the larger contact of power relations in society. Policies and strategies for future information societies must devise accountability measures that avoid the excesses of governance from above (top-down interventions and exclusively market-led development) and the excesses of naïve trust in commons-led developments (bottom-up initiatives and exclusively open developments). The outcomes, which will take different shapes in various countries and regions, will be determined by the balance which is struck between open, closed and hybrid imaginaries, policies and practices in future information societies.

1

OPEN INTERNET

The internet in LAC will remain free, public and open over the next 10 years

Hernán Galperín[1]

The internet is not open by nature. It is open by design. Looking back, its original architects often praise their creation as a visionary statement of freedom to communicate and to share information. In reality, openness was also an effective response to several constraints that existed at the time. Existing networks ran on different hardware and used different communication protocols. This required a design approach that made communication between networks (internetworking, or internet for short) independent of the underlying computing infrastructure. Long-distance lines were controlled by telephone monopolies which ruthlessly protected networks against foreign intrusion (Hush-a-Phone remains a classic example). The design choice thus favored the overlaying of a logical network on top of the Public Switched Telecommunications Network (PSTN). Funding was limited and computing power expensive, which favored keeping core network operations to a minimal (no authentication required nor quality of service provided), and delegating non-essential tasks to the terminals at the edges of the network.

---

1   Hernan Galperin is an Associate Professor and Director, at the Center for Technology and Society in the Universidad de San Andrés (Argentina). He is also a member of the Steering Committee for DIRSI, an ICT policy research consortium for Latin America and the Caribbean, and a Research Fellow at the Annenberg School for Communication at the University of Southern California.

The internet's openness thus not only reflects the shared values of the epistemic community from which it emerged (essentially US and Western European computer scientists). It also represents an effective response to the technology and industry constraints that existed at the time. The context in which the internet is evolving today is dramatically different. Computing power is dirt cheap. Telecommunications markets are fiercely competitive. And the internet has grown from academic obscurity to a pervasive communication platform used by billions. Not surprisingly, some of its core design principals have come under scrutiny, as they involve trade-offs that favour certain commercial and social outcomes over others. Openness often collides with many legitimate interests from businesses and governments - as well as with many not-so-legitimate ones such as restraining freedom of speech. Whether it will endure unscathed the next decade is an open question.

Defining openness

The internet can be defined as an open network as a result of three key design features. First, because its basic communications protocols are publicly available and royalty-free, and because the network is easily scalable, barriers to entry are extremely low. By contrast, many other existing networks are closed in the sense that entry requires entering into commercial agreement with whoever controls the intellectual property or the underlying infrastructure. These are private clubs, as opposed to the public commons nature of the internet.

Second, the internet is designed to accommodate heterogeneous end terminals and software applications. This results from a key design principle (called "end-to-end" or e2e) which specifies that the communication protocols must be as simple and general as possible, leaving all other tasks to end-node terminals –initially computers, now a variety of data-processing devices. To keep it simple, internet routers (essentially computers dedicated to delivering traffic across the net) pass along data packets (the basic units of internet communication) regardless of their content, using algorithms that maximize network throughput given the available resources. No promises are made as to whether data packets will be delivered to their final destination at a specific time or in a specific sequence. In fact there is no guarantee that packets will be delivered at all. This third design principle, referred to as "best-effort" delivery, is at the center of current debates about network neutrality.

These design principles make the internet radically different from the telephony network upon which it originally relied for basic data transport. In fact, the internet resembles more an electric grid than a telephone network. It is a general-purpose technology that, like electricity, "powers" many applications and multiple devices (such as PCs, tablets, mobile phones, game consoles, TVs, and soon refrigerators and toasters as well!). From a systems architecture perspective, it works more like the traditional postal service: the network operator makes its best effort to deliver anonymous letters to their final destination, roughly on a first-come, first-served basis. If a letter does not arrive in time or at all, you are simply out of luck.

The internet is also open in non-technical terms. Most significantly, it is governed by a loose structure of technical committees and non-governmental bodies that are essentially open to participation by multiple stakeholders, from government officials to industry representatives to end-users. This rather informal and non-hierarchical governance structure has evolved over several decades, maintaining cohesion around basic governance principles such as rule by "rough consensus". In essence, it is a system that favors technical expertise over representation of interests, rooted in the openness and meritocracy that characterizes the academic community.

Openness at stake

Openness involves trade-offs. A decentralized network with very low entry barriers and no embedded authentication is necessarily less secure than a network that centrally controls and authorizes entry. Interoperability between multiple devices and software applications is necessarily more challenging in an open network environment than in a closed one, where the network operator can clearly define end-device specs and hand-pick applications and content for end-users. If all data packets are treated equally it is difficult to make promises about quality of service for latency-sensitive applications such as VoIP.

The evolution of the internet from a research network that supported a limited number of asynchronous applications such as email and remote computing (where packets delays or loss could be easily tolerated) to a global platform for entertainment delivery and real-time communication is straining some of its core design principles. Video streaming alone, which demands reliable delivery of packets at high speeds, accounts today for about half of all global consumer internet traffic, and is expected to grow at a rapid pace over the next decade. For comparison, email and web data, once the dominant internet applications, account today for less than 20% of global IP traffic.

The profile of internet users has also changed dramatically. In the early days, it comprised a rather homogenous group of highly skilled researchers and technology enthusiasts, who rarely had to pay the bills associated with their fledging prototype (their base institutions took care of that). Today's estimated 2.4 billion users are as heterogeneous as one can possibly imagine. They have very different usage patterns; their skills vary from functionally illiterate to high-level computer programming; and while some demand an always-on, all-you-can-eat connection, others have a very tight connection budget, and may be willing to sacrifice control over their online experience in exchange for ease-of-use, security, or lower access costs.

User terminals and interfaces are also changing rapidly. While the internet was deliberately designed to accommodate multiple end-user devices, its initial growth piggy-backed on the earlier massification of the desktop computer under the reign of the Wintel (Windows + Intel) computing platform. The internet of today is increasingly about mobile devices, and Latin America and the rest of the developing world are at the forefront of this mobile revolution. The rise of the mobile internet is accompanied by major shifts in personal computing platforms and user interfaces. Global shipments of Windows-based personal computing devices (PCs, tablets, and smartphones) collapsed from over 90% in 2007 (the year the iphone was launched) to 35% in 2011. Apple's iOS and Android have been the big winners.

As the internet evolves, the design principles at its core have become the object of contentious battles. Service operators want freedom to create differentiated services, bundle applications and experiment with new business models that provide a more user-friendly experience –which may result in cheaper access, if they succeed in creating a two-side market in which advertisers and content providers pay to reach their broadband subscribers. Breaking-free from the constraints of the postal service model of best-effort delivery, they claim, will create investment incentives to bring fiber networks closer to the home and spur innovation in a new wave of integrated network services. It is also stated that more active traffic management and packet inspection could significantly improve network security, thus reducing the ballooning cost (and annoyance) associated with malware, spam and the like.

Similarly, the core design principles of the internet, and its increasingly global nature, often present challenges for governments to enforce national legislation, to combat cybercrime, to collect taxes, and more generally to influence the structure of the communications and information industries. Many policymakers long for the days when a handful of broadcasters held significant sway over public opinion. As Iran,

China and other nations that actively filter internet content have learned, the design principles of the internet make it much more difficult to reign on freedom of speech and information sharing. Moreover, many governments distrust the existing structure of internet governance. They advocate for the creation of a single, UN-like body that sets internet standards, allocates critical network resources (such as domain names and IP numbers), and sets the terms of interconnection between networks. In short, classic multilateralism, not the ad hoc, multistakeholder system of today.

A Latin flavor

Several factors distinguish the internet ecosystem in Latin America from the more developed regions. First, the average internet user in Latin America is younger, less affluent, more likely to access through a mobile device, much less concerned about intellectual property law (but more concerned about security), and less experienced with other information technologies. This sets different terms for the debate about internet openness. For example, users may be more willing to compromise a certain degree of control over their online experience for cheaper access and ease-of-use. Mobile operators in several countries already offer packages that bundle voice services with access to preselected internet applications (such as the most popular social networks and email services) at low incremental costs.

Second, despite a vibrant industry of local content and application developers that exists in many countries in the region, large international players rule in almost every internet market category (social network, microblogging, video streaming, web portal, VoIP and so on), with the notable exception of news, where established media companies have a natural advantage. In contrast, dominant telecom carriers tend to be local or regional, and employ vast numbers of people, which typically translates into political clout. The equilibrium of industry forces that has contributed to maintain the internet status quo in other regions seems much more fragile in Latin America.

Third, Latin American democracies are young, and some the basic democratic principles related to freedom of speech, civil liberties and privacy are permanently being tested in the courts as well as the political arena. As an open commons for political debate and the exercise of multiple freedoms, the internet is often the subject of regulatory efforts that, even when well-intentioned, threaten some of its basic openness principles. On the other hand, young democracies are often more capable of accommodating new issues and introducing innovative legislation. The internet neutrality legislation introduced in Chile in 2010, the first of its kind worldwide, is a good example.

Looking ahead

Governments and large businesses are often an effective coalition for change. Both have incentives to transform the internet status quo in ways that challenge its open architecture and its public commons nature. However there are also strong counterforces. Despite the presence of large players, the internet industry as a whole is highly fragmented, and many oppose changes to its core design principles, which provide a level-playing field to application developers, content creators, and device manufacturers, thus promoting disruptive innovation from newcomers. Many governments are wary about introducing changes that could strengthen bureaucratic controls over the internet architecture, and possibly legitimize censorship. And countless NGOs and individual users have embraced the openness cause. Today's equilibrium seems unstable. And yet dramatic changes, such as those proposed by several parties (and supported by several Latin American delegations) at the 2012 World Conference on International Telecommunications have been staved off –for now. It remains to be seen whether a new equilibrium will emerge in the next decade, and how it will affect the core design principles of the internet as we know it.

Free internet?

Pablo Bello Arellano[1]

The freedom of the internet is a conceptually complex topic of discussion. And this is because there is no single "internet freedom": there are many freedoms, some of which are even somewhat mutually contradictory. All (or almost all) of us agree with the principle of the "freedom of the internet" (along with the principle of net neutrality), but we may understand different things when we talk about it. It is a term that can give rise to more confusion than clarity.

One of the interpretations of "freedom of the internet" relates to censorship, in other words, any restrictions imposed on citizens –usually by governments– that limit their access to certain content or services on the net.

Freedom of opinion, freedom of the press and freedom of access to information (content) are not principles exclusive to the internet. They are democratic principles and therefore must be defended in all spheres of life. What history clearly demonstrates is that governments have been and continue to be the ones who most frequently limit the full and free exercise of these rights. In recent years, this practice has extended to the internet.

The push for increased government control over internet governance, advocated primarily by dictatorships in various corners of the planet, has received a surprising amount of support in some Latin American countries. Without a doubt,

---

1   Secretary General of Ibero-American Association of Research Centers and Telecommunications Firms (AHCIET).

the possibility of governments limiting citizens' free access to information and knowledge represents one of the most serious threats currently faced by the internet, and one that it will continue to face in the future as well. As such, when we talk about a multi-stakeholder model of internet governance, it is crucial to prevent a situation where some of these stakeholders are "more equal than others" –that is, it must be ensured that none of them has the ability to limit the free access demanded by society as a whole.

Internet freedom can also be interpreted as the freedom of users to choose the services they contract. This interpretation gives rise to an interesting contradiction. For some, "internet freedom" automatically entails a single type of connection: one that allows them full-time access to all services, applications and content with the same technical quality, a continuous connection at a single flat rate, which could also be referred to as "full internet". From this perspective, a "free internet" means the right of users to have this enabling platform at their disposal, without consideration for the cost or the use that they make of it.

But from the perspective of the users themselves, who have varying interests (and varying financial resources as well), "internet access" might mean using the internet in accordance with their own specific needs, such as using email or social networking sites or downloading a book on Kindle. For them, the internet is not an "enabling platform" but rather a collection of services, restricted and limited, that are the ones they use and demand. Establishing regulations that serve to impose an interpretation of what internet means based on a "maximalist" approach geared to a particular user profile (the single option of "full internet") poses a threat to internet freedom, because it standardises users and could increase the cost of services, thereby widening the access gap. We believe, on the contrary, that a model that allows users to choose which services they contract, combined with the possibility of opting for the alternative of "full internet", is coherent with the principle of the freedom of the internet. Regulations that limit the ability of users to choose the kind of internet access they want are a threat to this freedom.

Meanwhile, it was long believed that the main problem associated with internet freedom was the access network. This is of course an important factor, although its relative weight has been increasingly diminished by the growth of the digital ecosystem. The real threats in this regard are now very minor. Today, in Latin America, the risks of an internet access provider blocking users from accessing certain content are very slim, and require only very light regulation at most.

Chile, for example, has incorporated two important criteria in its legislation. The first is the prohibition of arbitrary discrimination. In other words, if a package with certain characteristics, for example, a package associated with a particular service, is treated in one way, another package with similar characteristics cannot be treated in a different way. The second criteria concerns consumer information, to ensure that users are able to choose which services they want and how much they want to pay. With these two criteria in place, relatively appropriate regulation can be established. A third basic criterion should be added to these two, namely a prohibition on blocking certain applications and content.

Along these same lines, it should be noted that the demand for capacity is growing by leaps and bounds, and the only way to respond to this demand is by increasing the coverage and capacity of networks, which requires more investment. This leads to the question, how can we create the conditions for this infrastructure to be available to everyone? How can the telecommunications infrastructure be appropriately remunerated? It is essential to build an ecosystem that is sustainable and just (for example, low-consumption users should not have to subsidise high-traffic users), but it should also be "free" in order to stimulate innovation and allow users to choose, given that the internet, its business models and even its technological foundations are rapidly evolving. The threats to the "freedom of the internet" that were identified at a given point in time may no longer be threats in the present or in the future.

Let's look at some other potential risks. Governments can establish certain regulations that threaten the freedom of the internet. This is the case, for example, when issues of intellectual property and copyright are addressed, and regulations are proposed that respect neither the right to due process nor the presumption of innocence. At times in Latin America we have seen asymmetric and restrictive regulatory models in which penalties are imposed without due process, without mechanisms that ensure that all parties are taken into account, and sometimes even through extrajudicial administrative channels. Regulations like these pose a clear and significant threat to the freedom of the internet. This does not mean that we advocate tolerance of piracy and illegal downloading of content; but we do stress the need to establish institutional mechanisms that effectively protect the rights of content creators and also, at the same time, ensure due process for those who may infringe on these rights.

Finally, although there are undoubtedly other threats, we should mention the growing relative weight in the digital ecosystem of large corporations devoted to the development of internet services and applications, and the risks that this entails. There is no denying it: companies like Google, Facebook, Apple and Yahoo! account for a major share of the public demand for internet services and applications, but there are a series of potentially complex aspects involved here. On one hand, the rise of closed, non-interoperable systems (iOS, Windows OS, Android) limits the freedom to exchange programs and documents, contrary to what occurs by default in telecommunications networks, which operate with standardised protocols that are designed to be interoperable. In the world of content and services we are increasingly moving towards non-interoperable models, where users enter into an ecosystem from which it is difficult to share with other spaces. This limits the freedom of the internet, which was created precisely on the basis of convergence and the use of integrable protocols.

In this context of monopolistic competition and growing concentration of market control, due to the network effect and the successive acquisitions made by the big players in the field, there is another issue related to freedom that becomes particularly relevant: the protection of personal information.

The personal information economy is booming. Users are offered services that are supposedly "free of charge" but are made profitable through personally targeted advertising and the selling of online identities. The question here is, how can personal information in the "cloud" be adequately managed? There are two problems here related to internet freedom. First, network economies limit the possibility of genuinely competing against the big personal information aggregators. Second, our freedom of movement in the world of the internet is curtailed, because our digital footprint is always present and the accumulation of information managed by the big administrators of the "cloud" is used to determine the services that are offered to us and limit our freedom of choice.

These are some –but not all– of the threats to the freedom of the internet. Others will undoubtedly emerge in the future. What we must avoid is moving towards a fragmented, non-integrated internet of non-interoperable islands, which goes against the ethos underlying the creation of the internet itself. The freedom of users to choose, the freedom of citizens to access information, the freedom to create and the freedom to express one's opinions are fundamental principles whose survival is not guaranteed. We all have a duty to defend them.

Risks and challenges for freedom of expression on the internet

Eleonora Rabinovich[1]

What do we mean when we talk about a "public, free and open" internet from a human rights perspective?

The internet represents a space that offers opportunities for political and social participation by individuals, and for the exercise of many fundamental rights, such as the rights to education, freedom of association, culture, freedom of expression, access to public information, and others. However, the promises offered by the use of information and communications technologies (ICTs) have brought serious challenges with them –to such an extent that the United Nations Human Rights Council adopted a resolution in 2012 which stipulates that people's rights, particularly freedom of expression, must also be protected on the internet. While the Council's resolution does not add a great deal in normative terms, it can be interpreted as a warning in response to the various decisions adopted by both governments and corporations that threaten the full exercise of rights online.

In Latin America, discussions around internet public policies and regulations have started to gain greater visibility in recent years, and the region, after a certain delay, has joined in the global debates on the issues involved. But this delay is not necessarily something negative: it has allowed us to learn from

1   Director of the Freedom of Expression Programme at the Asociación por los Derechos Civiles (ADC), Argentina.

the lessons offered by responses to similar issues in places like the United States and western Europe. In this context, I would like to take a closer look at a few areas where various principles related to the freedom of expression and the protection of other fundamental rights are being put to the test on a daily basis.

First of all, we need to address the inequalities in access to the internet. While many governments in the region have made considerable efforts to promote connectivity policies and programmes, with mixed results, the remaining gaps in access –which affect, for example, rural populations– have an impact on the equal exercise of rights.

Government responses to so-called cybercrime represent another area that merits a closer look. A good deal of the legislation that has been proposed or adopted, while perhaps well intentioned, threatens the fundamental openness of the internet and respect for basic human rights principles, such as legality (due to the vague or ambiguous definition of criminal offences) or the proportionality of the penalties imposed.

There is a recent example that illustrates how improper prosecution of computer crime can impact on individual rights and guarantees. In Chile, a young man was subject to a criminal investigation for the crime of usurpación de nombre or "usurpation of identity" (a form of identity theft or criminal impersonation). Why? He had been accused of operating two parody Twitter accounts that used the name of one of Chile's wealthiest businessmen. Satire aimed at public figures and on issues of public interest constitutes legitimate speech, protected by the right to freedom of expression, and the young man was finally acquitted. But the case serves as a warning signal.

Finally, the protection of intellectual property rights to the detriment of other fundamental rights represents a trend that could seriously affect internet development, openness and democracy in Latin America. Some of the draft legislation under discussion, particularly as a consequence of obligations arising from free trade agreements, has proposed copyright protection measures that compromise due process and/or freedom of expression online. This was the case of the bill for the so-called Lleras Law in Colombia, for example. Today, the secret negotiations around the Trans-Pacific Partnership (TPP) agreement –which include the United States, Mexico, Chile and Peru– have the region's activists on their guard, because they could result in systems for the monitoring and removal of "infringing" content by private intermediaries, among many other problematic aspects. The fear is that these negotiations will weaken the position of laws that adhere more closely to human rights standards, such as the current legislation in Chile, where a court order is needed to require the removal of content by intermediaries.

What can be done to guarantee openness and respect for freedom of expression and other rights on the internet? This is a difficult and perhaps presumptuous question, but this doesn't mean that we shouldn't attempt to put forward some possible answers.

In the first place, there is something that bears repeating, although it may seem obvious: policy makers and the courts need to apply human rights standards when designing public policies and regulations or resolving legal conflicts related to the internet. In this regard, our shared normative instrument –the American Convention on Human Rights– offers very generous protection for the freedom of expression, prohibits prior censorship, and stipulates very specific conditions regarding permissible restrictions (which must be expressly established by law, serve a legitimate purpose, and be necessary in a democratic society).

In addition, the joint declaration signed by the special rapporteurs on freedom of expression of the United Nations, the Organization of American States, the Organization for Security and Co-operation in Europe and the African Commission on Human and Peoples' Rights includes precise guidelines to be taken into account in the regulation of the internet. For example, the declaration states that internet service providers should not be liable for content generated by others, as long as they do not specifically intervene in that content or refuse to obey a court order to remove content when they have the capacity to do so; it adds that private intermediaries should not be subject to extrajudicial notice and content takedown rules. The declaration also defends the principle of net neutrality, and stresses that the blocking of entire websites is an extreme measure, which can only be justified in accordance with international standards – for example, when necessary to protect children from sexual abuse. The special rapporteurs' declaration is a good starting point for designing public policies and regulations that ensure respect for human rights.

Second, it is essential that those responsible for adopting decisions about the internet –such as judges or legislators– understand the impact, scope and even the effectiveness of their decisions as determined by the architecture of the internet itself. In other words, they need to understand what the internet is and how it works, and avoid solutions that are absurd, impossible to implement, or so disproportionate that they violate basic rights. For example, in Argentina, a court order to block the Leakymails website resulted in the "collateral damage" of the temporary blocking of hundreds of completely unrelated sites.

Lastly, civil society must devote even greater effort to the defence and promotion of human rights on the internet. In Latin America there is a very significant mass of human rights activists and organisations –many of them with long histories and sustained influence in different fields– who should be trained in order to become adequately involved in internet policy and regulation issues, working alongside and generating synergies with new organisations and activists from the ICT field.

Whether or not the internet remains open, free and public for the next ten years will depend on the response to many of the challenges discussed here.

2

NEW COLLABORATIVE BUSINESS MODELS

Defining the sharing economy for development

Fernando Perini[1]

In developed countries, where the presence of computing, the internet and other communications technology is pervasive, educational levels are relatively high, and societies are heavily oriented towards knowledge-based products and services, a growing number of examples of new forms of collaboration are emerging as a consequence of the spread of digital technologies. A new generation of business models –broadly associated with the concept of a sharing economy– seems to indicate that these new forms of collaborative business models are structural in nature and are here to stay.

At the same time, there has been rapid growth of increasingly intelligent communications devices (i.e. mobile phones and computers that allow access to messaging, voice, images, etc.) available to a large number of individuals in low-income and marginalised communities. The equipment and services associated with these technologies provide a valuable platform for sharing and allow micro-transactions and micro-activities at a relatively low cost, enabling coordination and cooperation among actors and institutions in a distributed geographical area.

However, most initiatives involving technology and poor communities have not focused on the use of information and communications technologies (ICTs) as a platform for

---

1   Senior Programme Officer at the International Development Research Centre (IDRC).

collaboration and sharing. The role of ICTs in low-income communities has largely being limited to issues of access and, more recently, as a mechanism to reach consumers at the so-called bottom of the pyramid (i.e. those who earn less than USD 2.50 a day)[2] or to expand the provision of public services, such as mobile-based agricultural information or distance education, bypassing traditional logistical and geographic limitations.

It appears that the potential of these technologies to facilitate new forms of community coordination at different levels has been neglected. The conditions seem to be in place for the rise of a digital sharing economy with promising repercussions on development. But little is known about the feasibility of this "economy" or how it may already be operating in informal settings.

What is the digital sharing economy?

The concept of a digital sharing economy is still poorly defined, and so far there is little agreement about what it means. It has been associated with open source software projects, creative commons publications, peer-to-peer music sharing, crowdsourcing, carpooling and many other forms of community-based collaboration enabled by technology. It has also been addressed in different streams of work. For instance:

Many associate the digital sharing economy with the idea of digital commons. Yochai Benkler coined the phrase "commons-based peer production" to describe how a large group of individuals work together in a decentralised way to build something strictly for the benefit of the commons. Typically, he refers to the creation and expansion of products of individual work that are available to all to use and modify, without any fees, often with the stipulation that any modifications will be made

---

2 Shah, Anup . 2013. "Poverty Facts and Stats" en *Global Issues* www.globalissues.org/article/26/poverty-facts-and-stats

easily available to others. Through a logic that defies traditional economic principles, open source projects and the free internet encyclopedia Wikipedia, for example, create value without the involvement of economic transactions.[3]

Larry Lessig, founder of Creative Commons, showed that there is a rapidly expanding part of the digital sphere (and our collective culture) that does not operate inside the traditional approach to intellectual property, and it is an essential part of modern societies. He demonstrated that sharing and remixing in digital communities are increasingly intertwined with commercial uses of the technology, enabling a new generation of business models that take advantage of contributions from the community while creating profitable enterprises.[4]

Rachel Botsman and Roo Rogers detailed the resurgence of a lifestyle of sharing, swapping and lending that is growing to new heights as a result of online networks and marketplaces –defined as "collaborative consumption".

There continues to be controversy over whether to include activities involving economic transactions or businesses which include a for-profit component within the sharing economy. However, exploring a wide number of cases, we observed that many of these initiatives are based on a different set of values strongly connected with "communities". Even when these initiatives included economic transactions and profit objectives, the idea of (and values associated with) "communities" tended to be the unifying dimension that brings this emerging digital sharing economy together. Based on different strategies and collaborative

---

3   Defined as "information and knowledge resources that are collectively created and owned or shared between or among a community and that tend to be non-exclusivedible, that is, be (generally freely) available to third parties. Thus, they are oriented to favor use and reuse, rather than to exchange as a commodity. Additionally, the community of people building them can intervene in the governing of their interaction processes and of their shared resources." www.onlinecreation.info/digital-commons

4   Lessig, Lawrence. *Remix: Making art and commerce thrive in the hybrid economy*. Penguin, 2008.

processes, these initiatives were significantly different from traditional market-based enterprises and state-led interventions.

Thus, the digital sharing economy is not simply a technological development. It is a cultural manifestation of an ancient and fundamental human (and humane) trait taking a leap forward based on the potential of new technology. We have always shared our tools with neighbours, slept over at the homes of friends or acquaintances, chipped in for community causes, given advice to strangers, or lent a hand to someone in need. As our digital lives become more intertwined with our physical lives, it is no wonder that many of these practices started to migrate to the digital environment. Now, people can use sites like Craigslist and Twilbee to find that drill they need in the neighbourhood. They can log in to Airbnb to find a place to "crash" while away from home. They can use crowdfounding platforms such as KickStart or Catarse to support community projects. If they need a tip or lesson, they can look at what is available on YouTube or specialised sites such as Skillshare. People can even volunteer to help out in relief efforts for those affected by natural disasters, for example, by improving virtual maps on StreetMaps or translating emergency-related messages on Mission 4636.

We could say that the digital sharing economy is the translation of a specific dimension of life to the digital space: our life as part of a community. It is the use of new digital technologies to catalyse practices, norms and values of our life as members of these social constructs. It is clear that these community values are very different from traditional forms of relationship with the marketplace. In many cases, we do not expect a direct retribution. They are also different from our relationships with the state: we are not mandated or regulated to comply with specific community rules.

However, although few would ignore the importance of this "communal" dimension of our lives, given its diversity and complexity, it tends to be ignored when thinking about the economy (as well as in the theories that guide our policies).

Is the digital sharing economy really an economy?

An economy is usually defined as the wealth and resources of a country or region in terms of the production and consumption of goods and services. By this definition, economic growth tends to be associated with increased production and consumption of goods and services. Most of the practices mentioned above, related to our lives as part of communities, tend to fall outside the traditional definition and measurement of the economy. We do not contribute to the GDP when we share a tool with a friend, give some time as volunteers, or even organise a garage sale. As some of these community practices move online (and grow in scale), we could say that they may even have a negative impact on the traditionally defined economy. For example, encyclopedia publishers are being forced out of business because of the volunteer-based Wikipedia, Airbnb rooms may compete with traditional hotels, and shared products may compete with new ones.

However, measuring the traditional economy solely in terms of production and consumption of goods and services ignores the undeniable value that community-based activities bring to society. Traditionally, this dimension was simply left aside when thinking about economic development, as it was usually comprised of relatively scattered actions, and most of the activities it involves would be sustained by cultural practices and social norms without a driving business model behind them.

The difference today is that now there are a growing number of companies and initiatives that are indeed building sustainable business models to drive these community initiatives in the digital environment. We have seen a boom in socially motivated enterprises that enable community-driven collaboration. These enterprises and NGOs are experimenting with models that adapt to the digital environment many of the things that we have normally done within the sphere of our social lives. Whether it is sharing a book with a friend, opening our homes, or donating to good causes, we now can find ways to take advantage of the widespread use of digital technologies to do these things in a more efficient manner. Thus, we could argue that unlike the past, community collaboration in the digital sphere does in fact need to be understood in terms of an economy, including a range of factors related to the collaborative production and consumption of goods and services.

There are criticisms that in some areas these practices go beyond traditional forms of collaboration and are invading traditional forms of economic organization. Some may even say that the sharing economy is a resurgence of socialist ideology.[5] But most would agree that there are individual rights associated with our life as part of a community, and that these relationships need to be considered (and regulated) in a substantially different way from our interactions in the marketplace. However, this border is not crossed in only one direction. The line between traditional forms of economic activity and traditional mechanisms of community collaboration is being redrawn with every innovation in business models. On one hand, private companies are seeking to take advantage of the dynamics of communities and are even promoting them in alignment with their business objectives. On the other hand, communities are trying to build sustainability into their organisational structures in order to expand their reach and impact.

Many cases show that finding the right balance between community-sharing value and economic-business value is often quite difficult. There are important cultural differences between those focusing on community-based versus market-based approaches. Finding the right mix may be quite context-specific, and it will require innovative designs that can balance different imperatives. Nevertheless, it is clear that experimentation is

---

5   "Don't believe the hype: Here's what's wrong with the 'sharing economy'" Milo Yiannopoulos 06-06-13 *The Next Web* www.thenextweb.com/insider/2013/06/06/dont-believe-the-hype-heres-whats-wrong-with-the-sharing-economy

exploding due to the value that this convergence can bring to private companies and communities alike.

What does this mean for the poor?

The rapid expansion of digital collaboration has started a revolution in many of the knowledge-intensive industries, including entertainment, research and culture. However, so far, it has not led to the same paradigm shift in areas that matter more for the poor, such as housing, food, education, water and income. Could these new forms of large-scale community-driven digital production systems represent a "disruptive innovation" that could help more people come out of poverty?

It is fundamental to keep in mind that most economic activities in low-income populations are related more to tangible goods and services than to digital ones. Thus, despite the euphoria of some over the power of the internet to change people's lives, issues such as housing, food and health services can be directly improved only marginally through the availability of information online. It is difficult to connect the significant value of collaboration inside the digital environment (where digital goods are non-rival) to the tangible world in low-income communities (where resources are limited by definition).

The long history of experiences with community development and market-based approaches to poverty alleviation also raise some cautionary tales about the sustainability of collaborative approaches targeting particularly poor communities. People in low-income communities often have longstanding experience in the development of a wide range of "self-help" or "solidarity" social organisations that include most of the elements associated with the sharing economy. Also, most of the economic activities of low-income communities are of a small (micro) scale. The nature of the scale of activities poses significant challenges in terms of achieving economies of scale to reduce costs, integrating different components of a production process, being able to respond to the demand of larger markets, and progressively moving beyond subsistence activities and local low-income markets.

Community development is clearly an important part of development, but it is also clear that many of these economic challenges cannot be addressed solely through collaboration within the community itself. The surplus available in these economies is (by definition) non-existent. Moreover, people struggling to survive have obvious reasons for being averse to additional risks related to long-term investments. Thus, there are many reasons for experimenting with hybrid models beyond a narrow definition of community-led development.

Finally, the widespread use of mobile phones in low-income communities and increasing connectivity to the internet does not necessarily mean that these communities will have "latent capacity" to contribute to the sharing economy or receive the trust needed to gain access to shared resources. There is a need to think about new ways of mapping latent resources and creating reputation systems, outside the traditional financial mechanisms. This can bring new possibilities for expanding access to growing digitally managed common resources.

For now, we know too little about the nature of this new sharing economy and its potential impact on development. However, the connection of community values and new business models shows great potential to impact on the quality of life for the world's poorest. Therefore, we need to start to seriously explore how we can harness its potential contribution to a more sustainable pathway for development.

What will new forms of collaborative business mean for the bottom of the pyramid?

Geoff Schwarten[1]

The sharing economy, still in its infancy, has emerged in the developed world as a result of hyper-consumption, over abundance, environmental concerns, economic crisis, and a loss of connection to communities. In addition, the technological advances, particularly the rapid expansion of internet access, have led to the emergence of collaborative initiatives that take advantage of the internet's potential to efficiently match those that have assets or talents to share with those that need them.

Thus, the digital sharing economy is a rapidly expanding force –a critical mass of new enterprises leveraging the power of internet collaboration to deliver goods and services in entirely new ways.

These new enterprises are now sprouting up all over Latin America, in some cases, at the expense of well-established business models, and they are driving a revolution in sharing. Barriers that were once considered impossible to overcome are now evaporating, creating a peer to peer economy never seen before.

Some examples illustrate the sheer size and effort of the digital sharing economy in LAC:

---

1   Business Manager for NESsT, and responsible for overseeing the organization's consulting efforts.

- US-based automobile sharing company ZipCar with 760,000 users and 11,000 vehicles was recently acquired by Avis Budget for USD500 million. While models for car sharing and ridesharing haven't quite taken off in Latin America, many start-ups are trying, including Carrot.mx –a "ZipCar" for Mexico– and Aventones –a ride sharing platform in Mexico and Chile. SaferTaxi, a mobile app in Santiago, Chile, matches nearly 700 taxi drivers with riders. These solutions will become ever more important as we try to sort through the issues facing our urbanized cities like pollution and traffic.

- AirBnB allows travellers to rent out available rooms, apartments, or homes, has had 4M travelers staying at 900,000 listings in 192 countries. (More than 20,000 of these listings are in Central and South America).[2]

These new enterprises are now sprouting up all over Latin America, in some cases, at the expense of well-established business models, and they are driving a revolution in sharing. Barriers that were once considered impossible to overcome are now evaporating, creating a peer to peer economy never seen before.

The digital sharing aconomy and the BoP

While it is clear that emerging business models based on collaboration are displacing long established businesses, changing transportation, democratizing the allocation of capital and more, what is less clear are the effects of these business models on the world's poor. As people in the developed world embrace sharing, and collaboration changes the way we feel about consumption, ownership, travel and a host of other things –what will be the changes for the base of the pyramid?

---

2   "Airbnb Celebrates Record Growth With 10 Million Guest Nights Booked" 19-06-12 *Market Wired* www.marketwire.com/press-release/airbnb-celebrates-record-growth-with-10-million-guest-nights-booked-1670787.htm

The base of the pyramid (BoP) refers to a diverse group of roughly 4 billion people (more than 70% of the world's population) that earns less than USD5 a day in local economic purchasing power.[3] A significant number of research studies argue that the base of the pyramid represents a sizeable market for multinationals and enterprises. When discussing the BoP, there is often mention of what CK Prahalad refers to as "the poverty penalty" –the idea that this group often pays a higher percent of its income to meet their basic needs for food and for credit. Often the poor live in rural areas where distribution or infrastructure is lacking, or due to a lack of formal credit history or collateral the poor are often denied financial services and "resort to loan sharks that charge usurious interest rates".[4]

Some initiatives try to overcome the financial difficulties of the BoP through peer-to-peer money lending, for example Cumplo, a peer-to-peer lending site in Chile, has lent nearly USD2 million through 350 investors.[5] Similarly, an estimated 530 crowdfunding platforms operate in nearly 40 countries, representing USD2.8 billion directed towards collaboratively funded projects and new businesses. Catarse, the largest crowdfunding platform in Brazil (see chapter 2.4 in this volume), has funded USD3 million in projects through its 150,000 users.

As with other developments in emerging markets, like the rapid increase of mobile technology leapfrogging the need for landline telephone infrastructure, it is highly unlikely that these business models and organizations will emerge exactly like those in the developed world. The needs of communities are different, as are the dynamics and complexities of the environment. A

---

3   Rangan, V. Kasturi, Michael Chu and Djordjija Petkoski. 2011."The Globe: Segmenting the Base of the Pyramid" *Harvard Business Review* www.hbr.org/2011/06/the-globe-segmenting-the-base-of-the-pyramid/ar/1

4   Constance, Paul. 2011. "A plan to attack the 'poverty penalty'" *IDBAmerica* www.iadb.org/idbamerica/index.cfm?thisid=4113

5   Gartner, Inc., a leading information technology research firm, estimates that the peer-to-peer financial lending market will reach USD5 billion by 2013. See www.gartner.com/newsroom/id/1272313

reality is that the poor already share and collaborate in their communities −sharing is not a new phenomenon.

Potentially the digital sharing economy could bring education and job training for millions, new capital to entrepreneurs and solutions that may provide health and security for families. Conversely, the digital sharing economy could also grow the informal economy and raise legal and regulatory issues that place new models against entrenched industries.

The following questions are posed in an attempt to understand the effects of the expansion of the digital sharing economy for the BoP:

- What collaborative digital solutions are emerging or might emerge to serve the BoP?
- Do these models hold the potential for positive social impact for the BoP?
- What are the risks inherent with these types of business models?
- How can interested parties like governments, businesses and development institutions foster the growth of the digital sharing economy at the BoP?

Cautious optimism and enthusiasm, stem from the fact that it is becoming increasing inevitable that the poor will be on the internet. The speed of adoption for mobile devices has dwarfed that of any other technology with now over 6 billion mobile subscriptions worldwide, and 77% of those subscriptions coming from the developing world. According to the World Bank, 90% of the world's population had access to a basic cellular signal by 2010. The World Bank reports that the bandwidth of these networks is doubling roughly every 18 months and expanding into rural areas.

The new, collaborative solutions we are discussing reflect an evolution in business models and methods of engagement for the BoP. Where previously some scholars had viewed the BoP as an untapped "market opportunity" for corporations to sell goods and services, the digital sharing economy brings potential for people to contribute, create and sell on their own.

Consider the example of education sharing site Educabilia. Educabilia operates in seven Latin American countries. What is unique about the site is not that it is a platform just for people to find classes and learn new skills, such as repairing iPhones and iPads, but that the site allows for nearly anyone to create and sell course offerings either through distance learning or in person. The potential that lies within the digital sharing economy is to unlock the skills, which are inherent and underutilized in disparate or poor communities. While Educabilia is not exclusively focused on the BoP, it is not hard to imagine how, given the right circumstances, the BoP might benefit from this type of offering.

In addition, digital collaboration allows for the creation of new digital commons – shared property that all members of the community can benefit from. In Brazil an organization named Rede Jovem noticed that widely used online mapping tools, like Google Maps for example, do not recognize and map favelas, the shanty towns where the poorest sectors live in many Brazilian cities. The favelas appear on the map as a dark grey area as if they do not exist. As a result, Rede Jovem set out to launch WikiMapa which, as the name implies, is a collaborative mapping tool where users can document points of interest through web, low-tech mobile and mobile web platforms (e.g., smart phones). Anyone can access, edit and map almost anything (streets, retail stores, public institutions, public spaces, sports venues, NGOs, hospitals and religious facilities), not only in Brazil, but also all over the world. So far, through six-month pilot studies of the WikiMapa application in five low-income communities in Rio de Janeiro, the organization has mapped over 1,283 locations through nearly 500 wiki reporters, and demonstrated a palpable increase in residents' sense of identity and self-esteem and new found appreciation of their neighborhood.

One more example worthy of discussion of how digital sharing and collaboration can meet the needs of the poor comes from a fast growing business called MobileWorks. MobileWorks contracts with corporations, educational institutions, or NGOs to crowdsource tasks that require human interaction like image tagging, e-commerce product labeling, usability testing and more. These projects are broken up into collaborative, crowdsourced "microtasks" that can be completed by anyone with a mobile phone and an internet connection around the world. According to the MobileWorks web site, "MobileWorkers come from urban slums and villages, from cities and farms, and from a variety of educational and professional backgrounds."

To summarize the three examples above, the digital sharing economy will enable the BoP to produce or distribute content, benefit from new shared digital "commons," and finally access new opportunities for employment and income.

Some proposed guidelines

So while the above explains the ample reason for optimism and enthusiasm, it is also possible to propose some guidelines for digital sharing solutions targeted at meeting the needs of those in poverty in Latin America:

- *Solutions must be bottom up* –digital sharing solutions that address the needs of the BoP should be bottom up rather than imposed from the top down. Providing the enabling elements, like internet access and platforms is very important, but the most successful solutions will emerge from within.

- *Potential solutions must meet critical needs* –the needs of those in poverty are immediate food, shelter, income. For digital sharing solutions to impact and thrive within these communities addressing these real life needs is imperative.

- *It needs to be mobile* –the current situation in Latin America is such that broadband penetration in homes is very small.

Mobile penetration will likely to be the gateway to the internet for a majority of the world's poor.

- *Not isolate but integrate* –digital sharing solutions can bring people into the formal economy through giving employment opportunities, inclusion into the financial system, and other aspects of the formal economy. Digital sharing solutions, if used effectively, can be a gateway to improved incomes and new markets for small holder farmers or producers of fair trade goods.
- Play the long game –finally, it is not likely that the poor will be integrated into the internet overnight. It will take an 'all-of-the-above' mix of the private sector, NGOs and governments to ensure that marginalized communities are able to reap the benefits of connectivity and that the digital divide does not add to marginalization.

Accelerating the collaborative economy

Albert Cañigueral[1]

The exponential growth of the internet has been transforming our economy deeply, mostly through value chain disruption in industries such as retail, media or communications. After the information age (connecting people to content) and the social age (connecting people together online), we are now at the dawn of a third age of the internet, where people connect online to share (things, experiences) and collaborate offline.

Collaborative consumption buzz and challenges

Collaborative consumption (or the sharing economy) has become an unavoidable buzzword on early 2013 to the extent that both *Forbes* (in January) and *The Economist* (in March) devoted their front cover to the subject. Investors are also flocking[2] into the collaborative space, and the interest is booming both in Spain[3] and Latin America.[4]

---

1   OuiShare Barcelona Connector, and founder of ConsumoColaborativo blog www.consumocolaborativo.com.

2   "Investing in Collaborative Consumption: Venture Funding in 2012" Stephanie Brincat 28-01-13 *Triple Pundit* www.triplepundit.com/2013/01/investing-collaborative-consumption-venture-funding-2012/

3   "El 'boom' del consumo colaborativo" Carlos Fresneda 12-01-12 *El Mundo* www.elmundo.es/elmundo/2013/01/11/economia/1357918514.html

4   "Collaborative Consumption explodes in Latin America" Albert Cañigueral 28 -08-12 *Ouishare* www.ouishare.net/2012/08/collaborative-economy-explosion-latin-america/

As usual, mainstream media attention helps to reach a broader audience and to raise interesting questions that early adopters and collaborative consumption entrepreneurs swept under the carpet:

- Our society is mostly prepared for corporations, purchases and individual ownership. When a new service proposal focuses on micro-entrepreneurs, rental and shared ownership it rapidly runs into legal and tax related problems. We are talking about social innovation therefore the collaborative economy needs its own laws.[5]

- Is the collaborative economy only for the privileged? Some have described collaborative consumption or the sharing economy as "an elite movement".[6] But there are also a lot of not-so-wealthy people involved in it. They are often the ones who run chores in TaskRabbit or drive the Lyft vehicles. How can we create a new collaborative economy that is equally beneficial for everyone, no matter where they come from?

- There is an endless debate about how money is ruining what started out as a transformative concept. "As collaborative consumption goes mainstream, it risks losing the very thing that attracted people in the first place, the unique and even transformative social experiences made possible when you interact with helpful strangers".[7] The flow of money into this space should not make us forget about time banks, cooperatives, credit unions, alternatives currencies, gift economy, etc. that have been around long before Airbnb

---

5   "In legal no-man's land: the collaborative economy needs its own laws" Albert Cañigueral 07-02-13 *Ouishare* www.ouishare.net/2013/02/in-legal-no-mans-land-the-collaborative-economy-needs-its-own-laws/

6   "Collaborative consumption is still an elite movement. We need to break that." Markus Barnikel 28-02-13 *Ouishare* www.ouishare.net/2013/02/markus-barnikel-carpooling-mobility-collaborative-consumption/

7   "Collaborative consumption is dead, long live the real sharing economy" Neal Gorenflo 19-03-13 *Pandodaily* www.pandodaily.com/2013/03/19/collaborative-consumption-is-dead-long-live-the-real-sharing-economy/

existed. At the end of the day it is about having a range of options to cover our needs.

From collaborative consumption to collaborative economy

I am an optimist and despite all challenges faced by individual collaborative consumption projects and the movement as a whole it is easy to identify an underlying trend far more relevant: the widespread adoption of the values of the collaborative culture.

Collaborative consumption is indeed the simplest entry point to experience the collaborative culture outside internet. Most users start experimenting with collaborative consumption for very practical economic reasons: saving or earning money.[8]

The fact is that any service or tool you use has a set of embedded values. Collaborative consumption services can be considered, to a certain extent, a trojan horse that helps plant collaborative culture values into their money saving users.

Collaborative values can not be limited to the consumption side and countless collaborative, peer-to-peer and open alternatives are reinventing the way we produce and make use of goods, resources and services, harnessing the power of communities:

- Makers bring on a new industrial revolution, driven by digital fabrication tools like 3Dprinters, facilities like FabLabs, open source hardware designs and "do it yourself" communities.

- Peer-to-peer finance fuels the system through crowdfunding, peer-to-peer lending, while proposing alternatives for value exchange in currencies and gift economies.

- Open knowledge is opening institutions such as governments, science, education and culture, while turbo-charging the overall development of all these initiatives in ways that closed alternatives can not even imagine.

---

8   "Study Finds Sharers Want Value with Meaning" Kelly McCartney 02-09-12 *Shareable* www.shareable.net/blog/study-finds-sharers-want-value-with-meaning

There is still little knowledge about the potential impact of these new models, and little systemic vision about the change they will bring to society and the economy: fewer intermediaries, less constraints, direct relationships –that being from person to person– inevitably lead to ahumanization of the exchanges, behind solely commercial relationships.

Many people, including myself, think that both for demographic and historical reasons Latin America is specially well positioned to embrace and benefit from the new collaborative culture.

Meet the OuiShare community

OuiShare is an open global community of passionate people (entrepreneurs, designers, makers, researchers, public officials, citizens and many others) working to accelerate the shift toward a more collaborative economy.

- *Offline.* "Meet people in real life" is probably the most important value of the OuiShare community. OuiShare connects local hubs to foster collaboration and new ideas, by organizing events all around the world, such as meetups, conferences and creativity workshops. Since January 2012, more than 40 events have been organized in more than 20 european cities. On 2013 OuiShare gained global traction with events in Buenos Aires, Rio de Janeiro and San Francisco. The first OuiShareFest was held in Paris in 2013, gathering more than 500 professionals.

- *Online.* OuiShare provides people from the community with a place for online conversations, and invite them to share their ideas and inspirations on OuiShare.net, the collaborative online magazine of the community. Launched in July 2012, it now counts more than 120 articles from more than 70 contributors, published in French, English and Spanish, all under a Creative Commons license.

OuiShare itself is a child of the collaborative culture that has been built on the basis of values such as openness, transparency, action, impact and permanent beta among others.

The only way to achieve such a massive distributed activity is to work on the basis of trust among peers and *stigmergy*[9] as organizational model. Quoting Francesca Pick, OuiShare Munich connector and co-editor of OuiShare.net, from a recent collective interview: "many members of the network have specific areas or projects they are responsible for such as our online magazine, a local community, or international events. But we don't have any bosses. Even though this can be challenging at times, we believe that the benefits of such an organizational structure outweigh the disadvantages since this encourages people to participate in the organization and develop their ideas within the community. When you put things into your community's hands, it flourishes and grows organically".[10]

Accelerating the shift to a collaborative economy

We think that moving the collaborative economy from the edges to the center of the stage will spread the associated values that have the potential to hack and improve the society as a whole.

The challenges to accelerate this shift to a collaborative economy are far from easy:

- The collaborative economy needs better exposure and education, which could fasten the adoption of new user practices, encourage policy-makers to support sustainable models, and drive business model reinvention by enlightened professionals.

---

9   See "Stigmergy" Heather Marsh 24-12-12 *GeorgieBC's Blog* www.georgiebc. wordpress.com/2012/12/24/stigmergy-2/

10   "OuiShare: Facilitating the Shift to a Collaborative Economy" Cat Johnson 25-02-13 *Shareable* www.shareable.net/blog/ouishare-facilitating-the-shift-to-a-collaborative-economy

- Too few of these projects are actually collaborating. Few know about each other, and a lot are still stuck in a competing mindset.
- Open knowledge and all previous experience shall be reused by those who are now discovering the values of the collaborative economy while enriching the global commons by contributing with their own experience.

Catarse and crowdfunding in Brazil

Rodrigo Maia[1]

About two years ago Catarse was born in Brazil. It came to the world as a reflection of the wishes of a small group of people willing to share knowledge online about what was at the time a strange and foreign word: crowdfunding. All of it was so newsworthy, and intriguing, and seemed to be the perfect solution for a kind of agony in which the cultural sector found itself in. I will explain below.

Brazil has a national financial support system for cultural projects that enables common people and companies to financially support cultural projects in exchange for a Income Tax exemption proportional to the incentive. On 23rd december of 1991, the Lei Federal de Incentivo à Cultura (Cultural Incentive Federal Act), was enacted. When it came out, at first glance, it gave the impression that the concept would work perfectly fine. Looking back nowadays, and superficially analyzing it, you could almost say that the law was based on principles very similar to those of crowdfunding. Taxes are widespread and paid by everyone here in our country. If common people had learned how to operate the mechanics proposed by the regulation, and if a better understanding had been facilitated by the government, perhaps the history of criticism towards the Lei Federal de Incentivo à Cultura would have been very different. But instead of it, the mechanism applied by the law has proven efficiency to be used for, lets say, other means.

---

1   Partner at Cartarse, first crowdfunding platform in Brazil (www.catarse.me).

Companies, mostly the huge ones, soon enough perceived that the best option would be supporting well established cultural products, from already well known cultural players in the country, and it turned the law into a good cost- benefit mechanism in terms of marketing. By applying your resources in a more "secure" cultural "investment" you could relate your company's image to a recognised project, benefiting from the marketing value generated by it. The lack of complementary laws ensuring a better resources distribution and directioning, associated with a slightly conservative mentality regarding the kind of projects that should be supported, lead to a process in which a standardization of how a company should direct its resources occurred, and therefore implicitly defined what kind of cultural products those resources would support. Companies turned themselves into gatekeepers of Brazilian culture. You can assume that implications of this behavior leads to the act of neglecting "risky projects", or the "disruptive ones", in order to avoid relating a company's image to a potentially controversial, experimental or simply not well known initiative. What followed is very predictable since that kind of conduct kills some of the most valuable aspects for iteration process and debates: diversity of opinions, a more varied nature of works being produced and exclusion of some points of views, usually the ones representing minorities, or delicate matters.

The explanations above are a brief and summarized portrait of how some niches in the cultural sector face the Brazilian laws for cultural incentive. And with all above being said, it is not difficult to understand why crowdfunding seemed to be the perfect fit. So, in 2011, we entered the scenario. We wanted, and still want, to disrupt the operating dynamics of financial incentive for projects here in Brazil. We strongly believe that Brazil's population has so much more to offer in terms of cultural, artistic, entrepreneurial and scientific products. In fact, we strongly believe that Latin America, as a whole, is so underestimated and has a huge unexplored potential. We don't want to deny previous systems, not at all, but we do really want to find common paths and pursue a less bureaucratic system and develop an agreement for how things could be done to enrich the iteration process and arrive at a better solution for all people involved. One that has space for everyone, and is divided by intense layering, where the communities, and niches, and a more local approach becomes more important and relevant than the masses. One where we could say that both newcomers and well established agents can have opportunities suited and adapted to their respective conditions and contexts. We don't know if it is possible, but we are working hard to contribute to this achievement.

And in order to change things that we are used to, we just might need to do things differently. That is why Catarse operates slightly different if compared to other companies.

First, we created a forum, to understand, have an idea, on how general public and enthusiasts perceived crowdfunding, crowdsourcing and other crowd related activities. The online forum made all the encounters that formed Catarse possible. None of the partners actually knew each other at early times. It was only an idea waiting to be hatched, that even had different names. Soon enough the three first Catarse founders, Daniel Weinmann, Diego Reeberg and Luis Otávio Ribeiro joined forces, with the help of the forum, with a complimentary group, formed by me and my brother, Thiago Maia. We were working parallely on other platform (Multidão, one of the possible translations for crowd in Portuguese). We merged Catarse and Multidão and the rest of it is what is today known as Catarse.

We are the leading crowdfunding platform in Brazil. We do not have the broader reach in Latin America, but what we do have is the largest sums mobilized if compared to all other platforms in the region. There are some key aspects that we consider pillars that lead us to our situation today. First, we bootstrapped ourselves. This was a measure to ensure independency, to give us the freedom to maneuver Catarse as we pleased. We sold cars, put money from our pockets and savings accounts, and, of course, we invested our own workforce without knowing for sure when we would have our return over investment. There was no solid way to predict how long would it take for Catarse gain traction. But it didn't matter. We were driven by passion, and willing to try it, with or without certainty of ROI. If our gut feeling was right, Catarse would be just the beginning of a wave that inevitably would reach Brazil at some point. Then, we made our most important choice of all: we trusted people and chose to pursue and open culture.

We relied on a very simple premise: By forming a solid community, one that really trusts us, we would be following the right path. If we really wanted to be trusted, we needed to trust first. Today, this value can be noticed all over Catarse's operations.

- Our code is open source, under MIT license. A lot of platforms are based on Catarse's code, some examples are: Impulso (BOP niche crowdfunding platform); Medstartr (health projects and fitness); Urban Kit and Neighbor.ly (crowdurbanism); We The Trees (environmental, education and social change); Nós.vc (similar to Us.you, a crowdlearning platform).

- Our roadmap and work progress are public. Everyone can follow what we are doing. There are two pivotal trackers available; Catarse Application (to follow our development progress and status);[2] Catarse (to follow our operational daily basis tasks).

- We really believe that building relationships is better than treating people solely as consumers. They can not be reduced to that mere function of consumption. They provide valuable feedback, they criticize, they can even turn out to be friends. With our core business, every person is a potential project owner, a person who can turn from a mere backer to a proponent. Thats why we try to expand our universe to offline actions, and that is why we are moving towards a co-

---

2   www.pivotaltracker.com/projects/427075

working culture since we are based in Estufa, in Sao Paulo state and planning to move from our office in Rio de Janeiro to a larger one, alongside with the people from Materia Brasil and their allies, who are piloting this movement.

- We work remotely, across Brazil. We have people in Rio, São Paulo, Porto Alegre and Belo Horizonte. All of them were crucial to spread the word and initiate local word of mouth strategies to acquire projects to the platform.

- We try to manage our people based on principles of autonomy, leadership and satisfaction. If you want to do something, agree or disagree with something, be my guest. But be prepared to debate. No bossy behavior allowed. The more collaborative and debated a decision is, the better. And this doesn't mean that everyone is involved in every process on going. Humans tend to organize themselves around common interests, and we only fine tune it to improve team dynamics.

- Regarding management, yes, we are emotional and we like to ponder numbers, efficiency with emotions, affections and heart. Continuous feedback is the golden rule.

- We are part of a major scope of initiatives, that naturally and organically gathered during the past two years. Engage, Imagina na Copa, Shoot the Shit, Simplicidades, Estaleiro Liberdade and so many others... We extensively trade experiences and share knowledge all the time. Comum is the most recent initiative of this kind.

- In a way, we want to stay small and lean –agile– and rely as much as possible on the network, empowering people to occupy some eventual gap that is noticeable within the ecosystem we are helping to form.

We see Catarse as a byproduct of something that is happening in the world. A kind of systemic change of mentality, that manifest itself through local actions and initiatives, and contaminates others due to the extremely connected world that we are living in. Maybe we are a few in terms of numbers if you consider a broader spectrum. Yet, all these connections forming between a large variety of nodes, ultimately, and perhaps unconsciously, will provoke a more generalized disruption. Who knows. We are following the road without knowing details about the destination. Thats why is important to share, and to stimulate collaborative attitudes and transparent administrations.

Despite the fact that Brazil is a huge country, with an immense territory, we try to empower people to deal with local issues. We do it via crowdfunding. This is one of the ways. And that is the point. We sincerely feel connected to lots of small groups, all of them dealing with their own local matters with the tool or mechanism. We can see, or maybe only feel, a rise of civil society awareness starting to grow in Brazil, and all over the world. Instead of relying on the government as a solution finder, we are empowering ourselves with this mission. We are responding to governments gaps creating services, new dynamics and proposing new visions of how things could be done. In the end, governments will have to make a choice. Probably, they will need to do something similar to what we have done. They will need to trust us, and act as supporters, assure our ability to experiment, to try, even to fail and learn from the process. Creating more bureaucratic barriers or trying to do things like the old ways won't help. We need to adapt, and in order to adapt, we need to trust. We really expect the governments to trust us. And by "us", I mean the civil society.

3

DIGITAL CITIZENSHIP

Citizen participation in the age of the information society

Valeria Betancourt[1]

There is no doubt that access to and use of the internet and other information and communications technologies (ICTs) have facilitated the exchange of information and led to new paradigms of cooperation, collaboration and exchange. Nobody questions the fact that the incorporation of the internet and other ICTs in public management as part of e-government strategies has resulted in improved provision of public goods and services and increased the quality and efficiency of administrative processes. However, whether or not these technologies have contributed to changing and improving forms of citizen participation in Latin America and the Caribbean (LAC) is still an open question.

Online citizen participation can be addressed from different, interrelated perspectives: the government-citizen relationship, cyberactivism, and online social interaction as a cultural phenomenon, among others. Numerous approaches to the subject are possible, and different authors and analysts have explored it on the basis of different suppositions. Here we will provide a very brief overview of two of the most important aspects related to citizen participation in the age of the information society: the government-citizen relationship and cyberactivism.

---

1   Coordinator of the Communications and Information Policy Program for Latin America (CIPP-LA) of the Association for Progressive Communications (APC) and a consultant for the project 25 years of the Information Society in Latin America & the Caribbean 2000-2025.

The government-citizen relationship

The redefinition and broadening of democracy in the countries of the region, particularly through new means of citizen participation in decision making on matters of public interest and the revitalisation of the public sphere, has been one of the main arguments used to promote the incorporation of ICTs in public management. The question remains, however, as to whether the configuration of power in Latin American and Caribbean democracies has been substantially changed by the evolution of the ICT for development agenda and the advance of ICT policies in the last decade. Numerous experts maintain that online participation is a reflection of democratic participation in the offline world, and that it is therefore essential to ensure mechanisms for greater offline participation and inclusion in order for ICTs to effectively contribute to the exercise of democracy. Others enthusiastically promote ICT access and use as a means to open up a whole new range of participatory possibilities which, even in contexts of democratic deficit, can provide a platform for voices that are deliberately silenced or sidelined by the dominant discourses and powers and enable the emergence of new strategies for social, political and cultural interaction and activism.

There is no single answer to the question, particularly when some political analysts in the region, who subscribe to different ideological tendencies, claim that Latin America is currently witnessing the construction of new models of domination, whose common feature (while not unprecedented) is the intervention of the public apparatus based on the "re-institutionalisation" of the state. One of the most notable characteristics of this situation is the cooptation, neutralisation or elimination of autonomous forms of social and political organisation and resistance. It remains to be seen if, beyond a handful of cases (which could be merely isolated or temporary, as in the case of online public consultations), ICT-based participation tools can lay the foundations for a new type of relationship between governments and citizens that moves beyond the hegemonic models of representative democracy.

The recent social revolution in the Arab world set new precedents due to the significant role played by social networks and other digital tools in organisation, communication and awareness raising. This could lead us to believe that the massive and innovative adoption of participatory practices based on the internet and other ICTs could become the seed for new balances of social forces, new practices of interrelation among different actors, and new configurations of power.

In any event, we should not lose sight of the fact that online participation (heterogeneous in itself) is not disconnected from offline practices and contexts, and goes hand in hand with strategies for access to information, transparency and accountability. We should also continue to promote the potential transformative power of ICTs for building equitable and inclusive decision-making processes. It remains to be seen if the open government initiatives that are emerging in the region point in this direction.

Cyberactivism

There is a vast and rich history of social, political and cultural activism in LAC. Resistance and opposition to the powers-that-be has been led by a variety of progressive forces, including social, popular, peasant, urban, community-based, students', workers', cultural, artistic, feminist and indigenous movements. These movements have struggled collectively to bring about changes in the political, economic, social and cultural spheres in line with their own political proposals and projects. In the early 1980s, some civil society organisations turned to the use and potential of ICTs to build and strengthen networks and communicate more effectively. However, it is not clear if these movements and groups have adopted ICT use to consolidate their transformative initiatives.

In addition, the collective nature of the actions promoted for decades by social actors in the region is no longer one of the most significant features of activism. The increase in penetration and usage of the internet and other ICTs, such as mobile phones, has opened up the possibility for individuals to spontaneously join together around the promotion and defence of a cause or for a specific purpose. This is as true in the region as in the rest of the world. There are countless examples of mass social and political action in LAC that have had concrete results and achieved important changes. However, it is less common for this activism to be sustained over time and to bring about structural changes (in symbolic and material terms) that are substantial enough to destabilise the status quo.

In "Ciberactivismo: ¿Utopía o posibilidad de resistencia y transformación en la era de la sociedad desinformada de la información?" we find this pertinent comment: "On the basis of the structures, mechanisms and devices of power, the usage, reception and appropriation of the internet and other ICTs have enabled the creation of alternative significative and existential possibilities. Although these have yet to advance to forms of emancipation, they have given rise to counter-hegemonic actions. In this sense, it might not be going out on a limb to say that universal internet access contributes not only to the production of alternative imagery and representations of reality but also to the generation of new forms of organisation of political and social struggle".[2] Nevertheless, it is not enough to project on other realities through discourse alone or to argue on the basis of the political meanings of cyber activism.

We need to find ways to put cyber activism to work for deep and sustainable political, economic and social structural changes,

2   Betancourt, Valeria. 2011."Ciberactivismo: ¿Utopía o posibilidad de resistencia y transformación en la era de la sociedad desinformada de la información?" APC www.apc.org/es/pubs/contribs/ciberactivismo-utopia-o-posibilidad-de-resistencia

so that they can be achieved in more just and equitable material and symbolic conditions and move beyond the globalisation of social struggles. Experiences like El quinto poder, No le temas al internet, Take Back the Tech and Marco Civil da Internet in Brazil, among others, can shed some light in this regard.

How we can deliver on the promise of open, direct, real-time democracy in response to current demands for citizen digital inclusion in Latin America and the Caribbean?

Sandro Jiménez Ocampo[1]

When we look at statistics on the expansion of information and communications technologies (ICTs) in developing countries, one aspect stands out as a significant challenge: there has been rapid growth in internet access in these countries, yet they are still a considerable distance from the developed countries. While the percentage of households with internet access is over 70% in the developed countries, it is barely 30% in developing countries.[2]

The so-called "digital divide" has moved beyond a matter solely concerned with media and resources to become an issue of governance. It has emerged as a determining factor in the development of social and political practices that enable or restrict the possibilities of access and social incorporation of ICTs in government-citizen relations. As such, the question of the sustainability and depth of Latin American democracies is no longer related to the use by governments of the latest technology, but rather the incorporation of technologies to mediate the issue of citizen digital inclusion.

The rapid advance of ICTs transforms the "digital divide" into a constantly shifting dividing line that creates inequalities between

1   Entrepreneur and founder of Kolaboraccion.Net. Masters in Social Development and PhD in Political Science. Academic advisor in open government and digital citizenship at the Colegio de las Américas.

2   International Telecommunications Union – I.T.U. Informe 2012

individuals, groups, geographical areas and institutions. Unlike other modern geopolitical divides –such as poverty, health, development– the digital divide does not follow constant, static patterns, but rather undergoes rapid mutations in line with technological transformations.[3] This means that, in the future, it could deepen or affect new groups who were not previously involved.[4]

These mutations, progress, advances or simply changes in the interfaces of digital technologies generate a type of divide that does not only affect populations typically considered as vulnerable. In recent years we have experienced such dizzyingly rapid changes that those who have succeeded in adapting to the incorporation of computer technologies in their daily lives do not necessarily form part today of the most advanced or successful users in the shift towards mobile, open and distributed applications.

In the meantime, the most significant challenge in this scenario is the growing phenomenon, found in the majority of current democracies, of political disaffection, as a substantial proportion of citizens distrust their political representatives or generally do not feel well represented.[5] When we add this to the situation described earlier, it is not surprising that the recent shift towards post-liberal political practices, characterised by the loss of the central role once played by traditional political entities, such as political parties or the state itself, further driven by the capacity for vigilance and mobilization of social intelligence articulated through Web 2.0 and Web 3.0, has produced an often conflictive confluence between the willingness of (state) supply and the exigencies of (citizen) demand.

---

3   Gill, Bernardi. 2005. "Derecho público y administración electrónica: una visión panomárica, nuevas políticas públicas" Anuario multidisciplinar para la modernización de las administraciones públicas. Sevilla, Instituto Andaluz de Administración Pública.

4   Duran, Francisco Javier. 2009. "Retos y Oportunidades de la administración y gobierno electrónicos" Revista Instituto de Estudios en Educación Universidad del Norte, No 10, Barranquilla.

5   Calderón, César y Sebastián Lorenzo. 2010. Open Government. Algón Editores.

Viewed as a window of opportunity, this meeting of disaffection with new forms of mobilisation highlights the priority of a new democratic opening, as a space for collaborative articulation of supply-demand-supply, in which the chain may originate from the government or the citizens, but must never be exclusive to the former nor exclude the latter.[6]

Given this scenario, we propose the following thematic areas, categories of analysis and questions:

Thematic area	Discussion question	Categories of analysis
Beyond the digital divide as asymmetry in access	How can we manage the digital inclusion cycle of access-appropriation comprehensively and sustainably at the level of both institutions and citizens?	Digital divide due to learning cycles. Digital divide due to cultural phenomena and processes. Digital divide due to institutional response capacity.
Institutional capacities for technological and social innovation	What type of new architecture in public institutions is demanded by the information society?	Capacities for evaluating the emerging social demands for direct participation. Capacities for public policy decision making based on predominantly participatory processes. Capacities for managing collaboration between institutions and citizens in real time.
The challenges of an open society: From open government to open democracy	What is the capacity of democratic institutions for updating their interaction structures to meet the demands for transparency and legitimacy?	The challenge of moving from participatory democracy to interactive democracy. The challenge of confronting the crisis of political representation for the consolidation of democratic digital mediation. The challenge of direct and real-time democracy.

---

6   This debate is more fully developed at: inclusion-digital.oui-iohe.org

Thematic area	Discussion question	Categories of analysis
The possibilities of social intelligence on new interaction platforms	What are the potential creative dimensions of social interaction platforms involved in political change processes?	The possibilities of political participation as a convergence of platforms. The possibilities of intelligent participation through the use of big data. The possibilities of a globally hyperlinked civil society .

This grid was used by a group of researchers at the seminar Open Development: Exploring the future of the information society in Latin America and the Caribbean (Montevideo, April 2013) as a basis for reflecting on the challenges of open democracies mediated through digital interaction, . The initiatives involved were the following:

- The project *Citizenship, collaborative technologies and regulation*, by Consumers International, a worldwide federation of consumers[7] groups with over 240 member organisations in 120 countries.

- The project *Analysis of the effects of cyber empowerment on the social, political and economic spheres in Latin America,* by Instituto Igarapé, a think tank devoted to evidence-based policy and action on complex social challenges. Its goal is to stimulate humane engagement on emerging security and development issues.[8]

- The project *Social media and citizen impact: Towards a new legitimacy?*, by El Quinto Poder, an initiative from the Fundación Democracia y Desarrollo (Chile) aimed at stimulating citizen participation and political action by offering an open forum for discussion and the construction

---

7   www.consumersinternational.org

8   igarape.org.br

of ideas that will develop into concrete actions both online and offline.[9]

To guide the conversation among the representatives of these different initiatives, a series of questions were formulated to explore the different ways in which each of them uses ICTs to enhance citizen participation:

Consumers International:

What is the civic action potential of the Like, Comment and Review practices of consumers in the digital environment?

How are "sound consumption" movements and new forms of digital citizenship related?

Instituto Igarapé

In what way does the deficit in smart data and capacities for its consumption act as an inclusion gap?

In what way is the production of smart data a requirement for smart citizenship?

El Quinto Poder

In what way does the creation of initiatives on your website reflect a new public agenda?

How is the representative-represented relationship modified through active mediation like that of El Quinto Poder?

How does El Quinto Poder affect the dynamics of social responsibility while being subject to them at the same time?

---

9   www.elquintopoder.cl

Social activism and participatory democracy: New opportunities with new technologies?

Hubert Linders[1]

There is a long history of social activism in Latin America which continues today, as demonstrated by marches for educational reforms, protests for the rights of indigenous people and women, strikes for better working conditions, and demonstrations for the legalisation of same-sex marriage, in defence of the environment, against destructive mega-projects, and countless other causes. But today, just like over 100 years ago, when a strike by saltpetre miners in Chile at the beginning of last century ended in a large-scale massacre, these demonstrations almost always meet with repression.

It is clear that today there is still not and there never has been much citizen participation in governmental decisions. The democracies restored after periods of dictatorship in numerous countries of the region are representative, not participatory. Every few years elections are held, candidates make promises, win votes, and then do what they want. They vote on legislation and policies the way that their parties tell them to, or let themselves be influenced or captured by powerful interest groups or lobbyists. In the meantime, citizen participation in legislative processes has been obstructed, usually by taking advantage of the typical shortcomings of large, heterogeneous groups, which encompass interests that are often contradictory, and have few (or no) resources to sustain an institutional presence.

---

1   Consumers International. The opinions expressed here are the author's own and do not necessarily reflect the views of the organisation.

However, information and communications technologies (ICTs) are becoming increasingly accessible for more and more people, and seem to offer new opportunities for social activism and citizen participation in government. The almost universal penetration of mobile phones, smartphones, and ever growing access to broadband internet –and thus to tools like websites, blogs, social networks, electronic campaigns, mashups and crowdsourcing– provide citizens with a great many opportunities to become informed, participate and assert their rights as consumers or citizens. In recent years, specialised websites have been created to allow citizens to voice their opposition to government policies through open letters addressed to the authorities with specific complaints and demands. Both individuals and consumer organisations have used these sites to organise and sign petitions requesting a wide range of measures, from the creation of a financial protection agency in the United States to the inclusion of more information on food labels to banning a harmful ingredient from certain soft drinks. Another example of this type of initiative is the campaign Water and sanitation are a human right!,[2] that succeeded in gathering more than 1.3 million signatures.[3]

There are also examples of websites where free and open source software is developed as a means of countering the hegemony of companies that place ever more restrictions on the use of their products by consumers who have legitimately acquired them, including DVDs, software and other products. In addition, there are web forums where individuals provide support for others when they are unable to install software that is available in other countries on their devices. This gives

---

2   www.right2water.eu

3   These types of websites include: change.org, gopetition.com, petition24.com and peticiones24.com, thepetitionsite.com, signon.org, elquintopoder.cl, avaaz.org, sumofus.org, causes.com, getup.org.au and twitition.com. I have created a web page where I have tried to include links to as many of these sites as possible at www.empodere.se/proyecto/index.php/ejemplos/ejemplos-enlaces. Most of these sites are in English.

rise to less legitimate but perfectly understandable practices, like sharing music and movies, selling decoders, etc., to counteract the intellectual property-related restrictions imposed by transnational corporations under the provisions of "free" trade agreements. This is also an expression of the general and growing discontent among people who are no longer willing to meekly put up with what the authorities "serve" them.

Meanwhile, as well as a place to post pictures of babies, pets and parties, social networking sites can also be used by organisations and individuals to express opposition to government policies or specific decisions on projects that affect their quality of life, the environment or the economy. One source of complaints, for example, is the lack of regulation on corporate responsibility to consumers. Many companies take advantage of this situation to ignore the demands or comments of consumers, since they can do so while continuing to operate within the "margins", often very weak, of what is established by legislation (when it exists).

When it comes to participating, however, a problem arises: there are so many causes that citizens are forced to divide their attention among thousands that they might consider to be worth supporting. And a people divided is a people conquered, as conventional wisdom tells us. The situation is even worse when political parties manage to "capture" or co-opt social movements that they deem to be useful for their own agendas. To gain a few more votes at election time, politicians may espouse the opposite of what they normally support: those on the "left" privatise basic services, while those on the "right" vote in favour of legislation that protects the environment and works against the interests of the private sector. The result is that activists are neutralised and their causes are made to disappear.[4]

---

4   For a good description of this, see chapter 3.1 in this volume.

I would now like to offer a few comments, observations and questions related to the risks and challenges facing ICT-mediated citizen participation.

Many governments talk about e-government as if it were the new panacea. But do they really want to change their decision-making processes and share their power with the people? Or would those who are in power prefer to stay where they are, and for everything to remain as it is? For example, there is now technology that makes it possible to vote quickly and effectively, almost in real time, even from abroad. Nevertheless, there are still countries with "arguments" for not allowing citizens who are not living in the country to vote.

ICTs could also be used to facilitate a referendum or direct public consultation on any controversial issue. But this gives rise to another question: Are we well educated enough for people to cast a real and well-founded vote on issues that are sometimes so technically complex that not even the politicians themselves understand them? And this opens up a Pandora's box: Should we assume that the people are ignorant, and that it is therefore perhaps better not to ask them? Furthermore, will we be able to count on the necessary transparency for participating in decision making on matters that will affect all of us in the coming years or decades? A good current example of government secrecy is that of the negotiations around the Trans Pacific Partnership (TPP) regional free trade agreement.[5]

I have the impression that the neoliberal model only works when it is able to maintain the status quo, that is, when it is able to maintain or widen the gap between the "haves" (i.e. those who have access to power, economic resources, etc.) and the "have nots". But the result is that people with less access to the internet, with slower connection speeds, with less education,

---

5   See: Cerda Silva, Alberto. 2011. "TPP castiga a los consumidores (y a sus bolsillos)" 5-07-11 *ONG Derechos Digitale*s www.derechosdigitales.org/2102/tpp-castiga-a-los-consumidores-y-a-sus-bolsillos

with fewer opportunities to demand their rights, with much longer commuting times, cannot participate in initiatives such as, for example, e-government. The so-called "bottom billion" –the billion people in the world who are currently excluded– seem to be growing rather than shrinking in number, and without the political will to promote the inclusion of the most vulnerable citizens, the situation is unlikely to change.

The same divide is found between those have access to internet or broadband and those who do not. There are increasingly more applications that make life easier for people who have internet access, particularly mobile applications. They can find out about discounts on goods and services, keep abreast of traffic jams in real time, etc. But those without an internet connection can only use their mobile phones to make calls or send simple text messages.

A recent IDB study on broadband as a catalyst for economic growth and social progress in Latin American and the Caribbean states that "a 10 percent rise in the market penetration of broadband services increases the GDP by 3.2 percent on average and boosts productivity by 2.6 percent."[6] If this is the case, why aren't governments investing or seeking investment to make broadband access grow more quickly, so that the country's GDP will do the same? Isn't it the government's goal to promote economic growth in order to improve the (economic) situation for the whole country? Why not define access to broadband as a human right, as the UN has done with access to water?

Another obstacle for more widespread use of ICTs is language: the digital divide between those who have internet access and can read in English and those who cannot is growing ever wider. The countries of Latin America should join together and find a way to create a worthy counterpart, sharing the best of what has been published in Spanish as open data. Access to knowledge

---

6   BID. 2012. "Informe: cómo ampliar el acceso y bajar los costos de banda ancha en América Latina y el Caribe" www.iadb.org/es/noticias/comunicados-de-prensa/2012-05-30/banda-ancha-en-america-latina-y-el-caribe,10006.html

means being able to read, understand and process information in one's own language.

In addition to the fragmentation resulting from the huge number of causes being promoted, as mentioned earlier, ICT-mediated citizen participation also faces the challenge of simple distraction. What is important now is no longer important five minutes from now, when the new Madonna video is released, the latest European football or U.S. basketball rankings are reported, there is an accident in a town thousands of kilometres away, or some actress wears a particular dress. The dizzying proliferation, spread and resulting overload of so-called "information" has given rise to what Lash calls the "disinformed information society".[7] Videos or calls for action go "viral" when people believe they are worth sharing, or because they are supported by celebrities with millions of followers who repost without questioning anything their "heroes" say. And sometimes there is profit involved.

A no less significant danger, which has turned into a business, is that of fake social network accounts. Nobody knows exactly how many there are, but they can be used to monitor the activities of individuals who protest more or less successfully against the authorities, in order to subsequently undermine their credibility through misinformation and defamation, thus hindering their effectiveness. They can also be used to counteract the social activism mentioned earlier.

There are celebrities who have offered to "retweet" messages for large sums of money, but there are also companies who can create more than 100,000 "followers" for just a few dollars. And these fake followers can sabotage legitimate actions by spreading misinformation.

An unfortunate situation is that with new technologies, governments can communicate directly with citizens, who may feel that they no longer need consumers associations like they

---

7   Lash, Scott. 2005. *Crítica de la información*. Amorrortu. Buenos Aires

did in the past. Through a great deal effort, some associations have succeeded in participating in decision making, and some have even gained representation in regulatory bodies. This position, which requires dedication, learning and knowledge of complex technical issues, could be lost as a result of more widespread use of ICTs. And this poses a risk, because in cases like these, citizen participation would be fake participation. People could vote, but about what? And consequently, what for?

Sometimes it seems that the internet and social networks are created for consumption rather than interaction. In this sense they are similar to free-to-air TV channels, which generally offer the public little more than "circuses". The difference between download speeds (consumption) and upload speeds (interaction) is massive, sometimes more than 20 times faster.

Another current phenomenon on the web is that of personalised filters.[8] Any type of web search on one computer will turn up different results from those on another person's computer, because companies like Google and Facebook now have so much personal information about us that they are able to "personalise" the results we see. If we want to see opinions that differ from our own, we need to look for another way to find them.

All of this leads to a final question: Are we really advancing with ICTs towards an information society different from current society, or are we moving towards a disinformed society, with new divides?

---

8   Pariser, Eli. 2011. "Ted Talk: Beware online 'filter bubbles'" *Ted* www.ted.com/talks/view/lang/en//id/1091

Smart data, digital inclusion and interactive democracy: Reflections on the use of ICTs to enhance citizen security in Latin America

Gustavo Macedo Diniz[1]

Smart data is a key issue in discussions around digital inclusion and an essential factor for the full realisation of interactive democracy.

This brief paper reflects on the importance of the intelligent management of "big" data for Latin American democracies, based on experiences in the use of new information and communications technologies (ICTs) in the area of citizen security. Although it is still in its earliest stages, the use of smart data in this area has been positive, because it has made it possible to: 1) improve understanding of the phenomena of violence and crime by the actors involved; 2) increase civil society involvement through a participatory approach to public security, creating synergies between citizens and government; and 3) develop efficient, decentralised solutions for the chronic insecurity in the region. We conclude by considering the challenges that remain for smart data to become an effective tool of empowerment for the people of Latin America, especially in the area of citizen security, and presenting ideas for overcoming these challenges, in order to encourage reflection and offer guidance for future initiatives.

---

[1]   Research associate, Instituto Igarapé, Brazil – www.*igarape.org.br*

The production and mediation of smart data as a condition for the exercise of intelligent citizenship and public accountability

To a large extent, the current crisis of representative democracy can be attributed to the difficulties faced by governments and civil societies (in a broad sense) in identifying, analyzing, understanding and addressing the infinite variables that comprise the social sphere in our mass societies. The polis has become too large, populated and interconnected for individuals, groups and institutions to deal with such a high degree of complexity.

The traditional methods of collective deliberation, including the method of our representative political systems, no longer satisfy the demands of these actors in the pursuit of their public and private objectives. We could say that the frustration felt by citizens today regarding the fulfilment of their demands (and not only by the state) is largely a result of the difficulties faced by public and private actors in interpreting and confronting the incalculable amount of data (physical and virtual) that is constantly being produced and transmitted by individuals and institutions.

The efficient use of smart data is a key requirement for this data –which contains valuable information on the society as a whole, precisely because it brings together a huge amount of individual data (obtained through crowdsourcing, for example)– to be translated into concrete and positive results for the individuals, groups and institutions of this same society. And this is an important step towards recovering the legitimacy of modern democracy: citizens only feel well represented if they see that their demands are being met, especially by the government.

In this regard, information societies differ advantageously from their precursors because of two specific potential capacities: 1) the capacity to disaggregate diverse and complex particular interests and attempt to satisfy the greatest possible number of individual interests, without the need to resort to the obsolete monolithic dichotomy of majority/minority; and 2) the capacity to analyse processes and trends –past, present and future, as well as in comparison with those in other places– or the design and justification of policies based on empirical evidence, although there may be resistance from certain ideologically motivated groups.

Thus, while the intelligent mediation of data currently offers an important contribution to public accountability, it will soon become an essential element of transparency for a new form of policy making, which will be guided to a large degree by smart data and greater collaboration between the government and civil society.

ICTs and citizen security in Latin America

Through the research conducted by Instituto Igarapé we have analysed many examples that reflect a significant move towards this new form of policy making. Through the Open Empowerment Initiative (OEI) –a joint research project with the SecDev Foundation of Canada, aimed at understanding the effects of "cyber empowerment" on the reconfiguration of the social, political and economic spheres in Latin America– we have observed an ever bigger role played by the democratising potential of new technologies. These have allowed civil society actors to make their voices heard and to become involved in areas of public interest that were once the exclusive domain of the state, such as public security.

Throughout the region, initiatives are emerging that use the internet and other digital tools, on fixed and mobile platforms, for collaboration and innovation in efforts to improve citizen security in the region. Latin America is the most "connected" region in the developing world,[2] but it is

2   In 2012, approximately 43% of the inhabitants of Latin America were online (255 million people), as compared to 27.5% of the population in Asia and 15.6%

also the most violent.[3] Citizens, NGOs and private sector actors are taking advantage of this first characteristic of the region to confront and seek solutions for the second. This is coherent with the principles of citizen security: a democratic and participatory approach to public security, focusing on the individual and the promotion of human rights, and no longer centred on the defence of the state, as was the common practice during the era of dictatorships (roughly between 1960 and 1990).

ICTs can be used to foster both citizen-citizen and citizen-government synergies aimed at the common interest of promoting security and peace, while enabling more precise and detailed knowledge of the phenomena of violence and crime (through big data analysis and research).[4]

---

in Africa (www.internetworldstats.com). Moreover, thanks to the shared languages and cultural traditions across the countries of the region, Latin Americans are among the world's biggest producers and consumers of social media, with particularly high usage of Facebook and Twitter (Diniz, G. and Muggah, R. 2012. "A Fine Balance: Mapping Cyber-(in)security in Latin America". *Strategic Paper 2*. Igarapé Institute. www.igarape.org.br/a-fine-balance-mapping-cyber-insecurity-in-latin-america).

3   While all countries and societies around the world suffer from violence in different ways, the scope and scale of organised and interpersonal violence in Latin America show it to be a distinctly more virulent problem here. For example, the homicide rates in Central America and the Caribbean are 29 and 22 per 100,000 inhabitants, respectively –two to three times the global average (Muggah, R. and Diniz, G. 2013. "Using Information and Communication Technologies for Violence Prevention in Latin America" En Mancini, F. 2013. *New Technology and the Prevention of Violence and Conflict*. New York: International Peace Institute. www.igarape.org.br/new-technology-and-the-prevention-of-violence-and-conflict).

4   See, for example, Monroy-Hernández, A., Boyd, D., Kiciman, E., De Choudhury, M. and Counts, S. 2013. "The New War Correspondents: The Rise of Civic Media Curation in Urban Warfare". *CSCW '13*, February 23-27, San Antonio, Texas, USA. www.research.microsoft.com/en-us/people/amh/cscw2013-civic-media-warfare.pdf;
     Monroy-Hernández, A., Kiciman, E., Boyd, D. and Counts, S. 2012. "Narcotweets: Social Media in Wartime". Proceedings of the Sixth International AAAI Conference on Weblogs and Social Media. www.aaai.org/ocs/index.php/ICWSM/ICWSM12/paper/viewFile/4710/5046; Coscia, M. and Rios, V. 2012. "How and where do criminals operate? Using Google to track Mexican drug trafficking organizations". *CID Research Fellow & Graduate Student Working Paper No. 57*. www.gov.harvard.edu/files/videos/CosciaRios_GoogleForCriminals.pdf

Equally important, citizen mobilisation allows for greater monitoring and reporting of abuses committed by state security forces (a historical reality that is still very much present in Latin America). In a recent paper, we explored the use of new technologies for citizen security in Latin America and categorised the different applications as illustrated in Table 1.[5]

Table 1. Vertical and horizontal application of ICTs for violence prevention in Latin America

Type	Approach	Functions
1) Vertical: government-government	ICTs developed by and for intra- and intergovernmental use	Real-time and social media surveillance and big data analytics for hot-spot mapping and internal accountability [data gathering]
2) Vertical: government-citizen	ICTs developed in cooperation with governments and citizens to enhance security delivery	Data fusion systems to enhance mapping of incidents and custom-made applications for citizen reporting [data gathering and analysis]
3) Horizontal: citizen-government	ICTs developed by private or non-governmental groups with applications for governments and citizens	Tailored open data fusion systems using a combination of ICTs that allow for anonymous reporting of actual or suspected crimes [data gathering and analysis]
4) Horizontal: citizen-citizen	ICTs developed by private, non-governmental, and activist groups for citizen safety and security	Social media and network systems using existing models (Google, Facebook, Twitter) or specifically developed systems [data analysis]

Source: Muggah and Diniz (2013)

---

5   See Muggah and Diniz (2013), op. cit.

There are numerous examples of each of the categories outlined in the table, which are becoming increasingly common in the region. Two examples of the third type of ICT use for citizen security in Latin America, based on the methods of crowdsourcing and big data processing and visualisation are Centro de Integración Ciudadana (CIC),[6] a platform developed by Citivox (Mexico) and Unidos pela Segurança (UPSEG),[7] developed by Stal IT (Brazil). Initiatives of this type and others are being progressively fine-tuned and improved, and are on their way to becoming a common practice that will help citizens achieve fuller, more effective enjoyment of their rights.

Conclusions: Deficits in smart data and capacities for its production/consumption as an inclusion gap

Despite the promising outlook, there are still many challenges ahead. These will need to be addressed in order for smart data to effectively serve as a tool for the empowerment of citizens in Latin America.

With regard to citizen security specifically, there is one particular problem that is the most urgent: the dual use of ICTs in the region. New technologies are not only used by human rights defenders and other activists to prevent violence and crime. Traditional forms of organised crime are also migrating online, while new types of illicit activity are on the rise precisely as a consequence of the expansion of cyberspace around the entire planet. This points to the need to strike a balance between the adoption of security measures and the preservation of freedom in cyberspace, in order to fight traditional crime and new technology-based crimes while protecting the anonymity of those who contribute to making both the virtual world and the real world safer. Today, for example, citizens in Latin America

6   www.cic.mx
7   www.upseg.org/mapa.upseg

are afraid of using ICTs to report crimes for fear of being traced, located and punished by criminals and corrupt police officers.[8]

In more general terms, a number of challenges have already been identified in the literature on smart data in relation to the digital inclusion gap. Because we do not wish to be repetitive, we will simply mention two interconnected problems that are pertinent to the current discussion and need to be solved:

- The first is the need to transform information into knowledge. This entails not only the promotion of different types of "literacy" (technological, digital, information, civic) but also the creation of platforms and tools that are attractive, visually appealing, interactive and easy to use. In addition to the democratisation of access, this will also facilitate the communication of complex issues. The Global Arms Trade Visualization Tool, developed in collaboration with Google,[9] is a good example. The tool aggregates data on international transfers of small arms and ammunition and presents it in a format that is "digestible" even for users with little knowledge of the issue.

- The second is the need to address the structural inequalities in our societies so that smart data can effectively serve as a solution, as opposed to further aggravating the crisis of representativeness. The problem is that the intelligent management of data depends not only on mass production but also collaborative processing of data (which requires giving people the right incentives to participate). Properly balancing these two aspects and ensuring that everyone has access to and knows how to operate and use smart data mechanisms are essential steps to avoid the reproduction of inequalities in a tool that should be used to eradicate them.

---

8   Based on the findings of interviews conducted by Instituto Igarapé researchers in marginalised neighbourhoods in Brazil, Colombia and Mexico.

9   See workshop.chromeexperiments.com/projects/armsglobe/

4

COPYRIGHT LAWS AND THE CREATIVE ECONOMY

Copyright Laws and the Creative Economy: How can science and education in the digital age flourish in LAC?

Ronaldo Lemos[1]

The debate about intellectual property and access to knowledge has been transforming itself quickly in the past 10 years. We are moving from the heroic phase, in which the contours of "access to knowledge" had to be defined (or at least clarified), to a more pragmatic context in which specific problems have to be solved.

Ten years ago, issues like e-health, e-education and e-government were more products of wishful thinking than ideas with a real possibility of being implemented in most Latin American countries. Conversely, the present moment has become a turning point for the region in terms of connectivity. Government policies, markets and non-profit initiatives are contributing to improve the overall connectivity in the region.

By 2012, 98% of the population in the region had access to a mobile cell signal and 84% of households subscribe to some type of mobile service, according to a World Bank report. This rather quick expansion of ICTs in Latin America and the Caribbean (LAC) caught many intellectual property and access to knowledge scholars and practitioners unprepared. While they were still considering hypothetical models for deploying and using information and communication technologies

---

1   Director and founder of the Center of Technology and Society at the Fundação Getulio Vargas (FGV) in Rio de Janeiro, Brazil. He is also a fellow at the Center for Information Technology Policy at Princeton University.

(ICTs), a significant portion of the region's population was already putting in practice innovative uses to newly available technology, and going beyond expectations in terms of self-organization and empowerment.

Examples include the emergence and expansion of cultural scenes in various LAC countries, tilting the symbolic balance from a centralized "one to many" to a decentralized "many to many" form of cultural production. Web services like Youtube or 4shared, created the conditions to disseminate cultural artifacts head to head with the mainstream forms of culture. Previously invisible voices from the region's peripheries were thus empowered by tools like social networks and torrents, by-passing the traditional media channels.

Moreover, the economic constraints surrounding connectivity also led to innovative strategies, such as the emergence of lan-houses, cybercafés that emerged in poor areas of the region (and prominently in Brazil) where a single internet connection could be shared in exchange for a small amount of money by a group of people connected by means of a set of computers arranged in a "local area network". Other arrangements include the emergence of a secondary market for cell phone "minutes", a direct result of the fact that more than 80% of cell phones in the region are "pre-paid".

Also important, the enormous potential of this low income market resonated even in hardware design and manufacturing. Asian companies realized the huge demand on the part of the poor for cell phones and started to design and sell inexpensive products, designed for low income populations. These include, for example, cell phones that cost USD20 and are capable of using four simultaneous sim-cards, allowing the user to switch between different carriers in order to enjoy the lowest fares and seasonal promotions, and cell phones capable of receiving radio and tv signals over the air, something highly valued by large parts of the population living in underprivileged areas.

Of course all these rapid changes and the new social practices they introduce clash with traditional forms of intellectual property and other established norms. The dissemination of culture through social networks or by means of torrents, in many cases, violates copyright laws. The use of "remix" as a form of expression, in which cultural artifacts are endlessly appropriated and transformed in order to embed new ideas, has become a central form of expression by the connected low income populations. Also, the cheap cell phones used in the shantytowns of many LAC cities are manufactured in violation of a number of established patents or do not comply with the certification standards of national telecommunications regulatory agencies. One of the challenges ahead is precisely to better understand the disconnection between the legal and regulatory system, and the connectivity practices of the majority of the region's population.

While cell phones have so far been the centerpiece of recent debate about the digital divide, a new challenge is emerging for researchers, policy makers and practitioners: to anticipate the impact of the increasing number of tablets. A powerful signal of their relevance comes from Brazil. In late 2011, the country had 200,000 tablets but by late 2012, that number had exploded to 5 million, with more than 50% of them being low-cost tablets of unknown brands (mostly manufactured in China), purchased by low-income populations that do not have the resources (or do not want) to acquire top-tier brands like Apple or Samsung.

In the same way that many people in the region purchased a cell phone without ever having had a fixed phone line, we are now witnessing a moment in which a large number of people are buying a tablet, without ever having had a computer.

This "straight to tablet" movement will raise a number of questions and challenges. What will be the content that is going to be accessed through them? Certainly it will not be books downloaded from Amazon, or movies purchased through iTunes –both are too expensive for low income families in the region that cannot afford to pay USD8 for a book or USD1 for one single music track.

Also, e-education might become a crucial issue. In the next 10 years, tablets will become increasingly present in classrooms. This raises questions such as what will be the copyright policies regarding such educational materials? or how will the transition to multimedia learning materials happen in the region? If classroom materials start to include films or music, collecting societies that charge royalties for the public performance of copyrighted works will certainly want collect fees from schools. If music is performed in public spaces, be they schools or ballrooms, copyright royalties are due and must be collected. The next few years will show whether the transition to multimedia learning materials in schools will represent another clash between intellectual property and social practices.

In sum, the issues that face us over the next few years will have tremendous impact for our societies and intellectual property researchers, educators, industry, policymakers and will all have to be prepared to anticipate the technological changes that are rapidly transforming the ecology of access in Latin America and the Caribbean. Ingnoring them will not only hamper innovation in the region, but also keep vast parts of the LAC population living somewhere between the formal and the informal world. That creates a vast class of citizens that cannot fully benefit from the expanding access to ICTs without the stigma of illegality.

International regulatory threats and institutional challenges for access to digital content in Latin America

Joana Varon[1]

While information and communications technologies (ICTs) offer huge potential to bridge developmental gaps by providing access to knowledge in a way never seen before in the history of humanity, there are significant regulatory constraints and institutional challenges that jeopardise this potential.

These threats are particularly intense in Latin America and other regions where developing or emerging economies are pressured by developed countries and the (national and international) content industry to meet a higher level of enforcement of intellectual property rights. This kind of pressure not only disregards the exceptions and limitations established in international treaties, but also runs counter to new internet practices that are emerging in the region. Even worse, this is happening in a non-transparent manner, bypassing the usual multilateral forums for international negotiation and, particularly in the field of copyright enforcement, raising questions about which institutional arrangements for internet governance can ensure access to content and freedom of expression.

Although the internet was conceived in an environment characterised by openness, sharing and a free flow of information, these internet rights and principles are facing

---

1   Researcher from the Center for Technology and Society (CTS) at Fundação Getulio Vargas (FGV), Brazil.

significant challenges with lasting consequences for social and economic development in the region.

The World Trade Organization (WTO) agreement on Trade-Related Aspects of Intellectual Property Rights (TRIPS) promoted the harmonisation of intellectual property (IP) law and set the foundations for the enforcement of IP rights worldwide. This approach has been criticised as ultimately promoting a flow of resources to developed countries, in the form of increased payments for copyrights and patents.

In order to balance this approach, an important milestone was set in 2007 by the adoption of the Development Agenda at the World Intellectual Property Organization (WIPO), as an effort to refocus the IP debate away from promoting stronger blanket protection to considering how IP regimes affect incentives for local creativity.

Initially proposed by Brazil and Argentina, the original document argued that "intellectual property protection cannot be seen as an end itself, nor can the harmonization of intellectual property law lead to higher protection standards in all countries, irrespective of their levels of development." As a result, the Development Agenda consists of 45 recommendations to member states. Technology transfer, ICTs and access to knowledge in the development context are among the issues addressed, and recommendation 27 in particular calls for "facilitating intellectual property-related aspects of ICT for growth and development."

However, despite the progress achieved through the approval of the Development Agenda, little else has changed at WIPO. Although they have been empowered by the proposals of the Development Agenda and by the increasing bargaining power of emerging economies, such as Brazil and India, developing countries face a huge lobby from the IP industry, nationally and internationally, which prevents them from setting an IP agenda focused on the public interest. An example of this stagnant situation can be found in the process for approving a treaty aimed at improving access to knowledge for the visually impaired. Even though the proposed treaty would be based on fundamental human rights and clearly framed under exceptions and limitations to copyright protection, no text has been approved after three years of debate.

As the debates between those advocating stricter enforcement of IP and those seeking to balance copyright with the public interest have stagnated within the multilateral system, developed countries have searched for other mechanisms to pursue their agenda.

In Latin America, the role of "enforcer" is particularly played by the United States. Every year the Office of the United States Trade Representative (USTR) releases a Special 301 report, well known among advocates for access to knowledge. This report establishes a blacklist of countries considered by the USTR to be on the "Priority Watch List" for having inadequate IP laws or enforcement. This "judgment" is assessed by standards that are even higher than those established by the TRIPS agreement and feature a "one-size-fits-all approach" to evaluating foreign models of IP protection. Brazil, for instance, regularly finds itself on the blacklist, either due to allowing photocopies of educational material at universities, or, more recently, to proposals for copyright reform and internet legislation on internet service provider (ISP) liability and procedures for content removal.

At the international level, the US has been pushing for trade agreements outside of the regular multilateral forums, using secrecy and a lack of transparency to set higher standards for enforcement of IP rights. Such was the case of the Anti-Counterfeiting Trade Agreement (ACTA), a treaty with substantial potential to inflict damage on internet regulations based on a human rights framework and on balanced copyright enforcement policies.

ACTA has already been signed by the US, Australia, Canada, Japan, Morocco, New Zealand, Singapore, South Korea and

Mexico, and was the focus of major controversy in the European Union, where it was finally rejected in the European Parliament in 2012. Even though Mexico is the only Latin American country that has signed ACTA, the US, pressured by the copyright industry, has not relented and continues to push for similar regulations and standards for the region, for example, through the Trans-Pacific Partnership (TPP).

TPP is a trade agreement proposed by the US government with countries of the Pacific region, including Australia, Brunei, Canada, Chile, Japan, Malaysia, Mexico, New Zealand, Peru, Singapore and Vietnam. Its provisions include restrictive measures for enforcing copyright and patent protection which go even beyond those proposed in ACTA.

Among its possible consequences are the extension of the term for copyright protection, an increase in prices of cultural goods and medicines, and disconnection of internet providers who do not enforce it, as well as criminal charges with penalties that could include imprisonment and severe fines.

Last, but not least, besides criminalising regular users and hindering access to knowledge, TPP provisions include blocking online content without a judicial order and a "notice and takedown" approach. This approach could create a "chilling effect" over access to content and freedom of speech, mostly because this system has been frequently abused by copyright holders and even by users willing to suppress freedom of speech.

If TPP sets such a standard, it will serve as international pressure, even beyond the Pacific region, for adopting restrictive measures in disregard of the public interest and developmental concerns. For instance, Brazil has already begun to discuss the implementation of the "notice and takedown" system; having such bad practice in the neighbourhood would definitely not help.

Thinking forward

In a context where developed countries are using trade agreements to impose international standards for intermediary liability and other internet policy issues, there is an issue that tends to be ignored by the access to knowledge movement: the need to address the international institutional gap with regard to internet policies.

As long as there is an institutional vacuum for internet governance, non-transparent and unbalanced regulations will continue to emerge, proposing damaging online enforcement of copyright protection. And existing institutions that already deal with ICTs, such as the International Telecommunication Union (ITU), will seek to fill this void. Besides the non-multi-stakeholder governance model of this organisation, this also represents a major risk of creating excessive liability of intermediaries at the infrastructure level of the network, in order to unduly deal with the content level. This in turn could result, for instance, in severe content blocking and censorship.

A multi-stakeholder approach to internet governance, in which governments, companies, civil society, academia and the technical community can discuss and decide on an equal footing, is a basic requirement to block extreme international initiatives on copyright enforcement and other threats to digital rights. This issue has been on the forefront of the debates within the Internet Governance Forum and should be on the radar of governments and academics and activists dedicated to promoting access to knowledge.

Nevertheless, the internet governance debate has also evolved towards a clear understanding that the right to access content is interconnected with the right of freedom of expression and, ultimately, with the right to development. Frank La Rue, the UN Special Rapporteur on the promotion and protection of the right to freedom of opinion and expression has made an enormous contribution to such an approach. He defines freedom of expression as "the right of all individuals to seek, receive and impart information and ideas of all kinds through any means possible." This definition is clearly related to debates on access to content and takes into consideration the availability and diversity of online content, not only in terms of what is accessible to whom (consumption), but also in terms of the freedom to create content (production) and the equality of treatment of different content as it is distributed through the networks (distribution). These dimensions of access to content are closely related to ensuring other internet rights and principles, such as the right to privacy and the principle of net neutrality, all of them broadly related to the right to freedom of expression.

Thus, the debate on access to content should always be framed in this broader perspective to promote knowledge and, ultimately, innovative solutions. And international regulatory threats and institutional challenges to promoting access to digital content in Latin America should also consider human rights and public interest approaches, as they are related to the right to develop.

The region has already promoted this type of approach, particularly during the meetings of the first Global Congress on Intellectual Property and the Public Interest, held in Washington, DC in 2011. The gathering represented the beginning of linkages among international civil society and some governments for advancing a positive agenda for intellectual property, considering, among other aspects, open business models, implementation and expansion of exceptions and limitations, and acknowledgement of new practices that technology has enabled.

Latin American academics and advocates have been among the leading actors in this global agenda which emerged in Washington in 2011. On that occasion, over a thousand experts signed the Washington Declaration on Intellectual Property and the Public Interest, which recommends an evidence-based path for advancing a more balanced regime for fostering science, education and innovation in the digital age. The second edition of the Congress was held in Rio de Janeiro in December 2012 and was a key moment for bringing together Latin American academia and civil society interested in this positive agenda.

While the pressures for unjustified restriction of access to digital content and threats to digital openness are growing, it is encouraging to see that civil society is engaged and becoming more organised and coordinated across the region. Connecting this movement with the debates on internet governance and human rights offers some possible paths to address regulatory threats and institutional challenges to access to content, in order to fully harness the potential of the internet for education, science and technology in Latin America.

Scientific articles in Latin America and the Caribbean: Is it possible to think of approaches that emphasise access?[1]

Carolina Botero[2]

Access to knowledge is traditionally associated with access to two products that result from the investment that societies make in science, technology and innovation: scientific articles that present research findings and are published in peer-reviewed scientific journals, and industrial property rights (patents). This paper offers a brief reflection on how to tackle the challenge, in Latin American and the Caribbean (LAC), of disseminating the knowledge that is created in the region and circulated through scientific publications. It also considers the importance of promoting public policies that specifically address access to knowledge, given the potential impact of the outcomes of scientific research on the region's development.

---

1   This paper presents the author's reflections around her role as a consultant for the regional strategy promoted by the science, technology and innovation authorities in nine Latin American countries together with their national research and education networks, with financing from the IDB. This strategy resulted in the birth in 2012 of LA Referencia. LA Referencia is a federated network of institutional repositories that gathers together the quality scientific production of higher education institutions and research centres of the region's countries, which are the nodes of the network.

2   Lawyer, and coleader of Creative Commons, Colombia since 2004. Fundación Karisma, Colombia – www.karisma.org.co

Public policies in the region have focused on production

A recent UNESCO report on national science, technology and innovation systems in LAC[3] found that, despite the efforts made in the countries of the region during the 20th century to influence public policies and enhance scientific production, greater work is still needed when it comes to the dissemination of scientific knowledge produced in the region[4] and its circulation through scientific publications.[5] This points to the need to move past the traditional model of the dissemination of scientific knowledge in order to increase its impact. Open access is aimed at placing entire texts on the internet, making them publicly available and free of charge for anyone to read, download, copy, distribute, print, search or link, with no financial, legal or technical barriers. The promotion of this type of access could be an innovative public policy response to the need for greater dissemination and circulation of knowledge.

Up until now, the trend in terms of incentives for scientific publishing has focused on the production chain. This has led to the promotion of the creation of groups of scientists and compliance with international standards in the publication of research findings. There have also been efforts to promote and facilitate

---

3   Lemarchand, G. (ed). 2010. *Sistemas nacionales de ciencia, tecnología e innovación en América Latina y el Caribe.* UNESCO. Montevideo. www.vinv.ucr.ac.cr/docs/divulgacion-ciencia/libros-y-tesis/sistem-nacion-cyt.pdf

4   "Ten years after Budapest, the highest rate of generation and absorption of scientific and technological knowledge continues to be concentrated in the developed countries. This has contributed to increasing the technological gap between the latter and those countries that are still developing. It was also acknowledged that stepping up globalized relations and internationalization of scientific and technological production *continues to be limited by restrictions in circulation and dissemination of the knowledge produced*" (emphasis ours).

5   Articles published in indexed journals and registered patents are outcomes of investment in science, technology and innovation that make it possible to measure and internationally compare a country's level of development in a particular field. As such, they serve to assess the country's general performance and are used as indicators of development.

the emergence of journals that implement standards of quality for the articles published through a differential measurement system that uses the measurement of impact. Other efforts have included the adoption of schemes for internationalisation, the development of systems to measure scientific production, the creation of post-graduate programmes, and the promotion of recognition of scientific production by universities through systems of incentives for lecturers and researchers, among others. Actions like these have served to improve outcomes in different countries; for example, they have helped to raise Colombia to fifth place in terms of scientific production per country in the region.[6]

While public policy processes around science, technology and innovation in LAC have focused on promoting the production of knowledge, the dissemination of this knowledge depends on foreign mechanisms of evaluation and circulation. This has essentially entailed the adaptation to the digital environment of the printed publication model –a model that is in crisis, as recognised by scientists and libraries themselves–[7] or to individual efforts that do not take full advantage of the dissemination capacity of information and communications technologies (ICTs) or the possibilities for discovery offered by the internet. They also do not generate reflection around the opportunities for access offered by the legal environment or the source of resources that make the creation of knowledge possible.[8]

---

6   SCImago. 2007. *SJR — SCImago Journal & Country Rank*. www.scimagojr.com

7   Although this is an issue that has been repeatedly addressed in recent years, this article situates the debate in a highly current context: "Harvard Library to faculty: we're going broke unless you go open access". Cory Doctorow 23-04-12 *Boing Boing* www.boingboing.net/2012/04/23/harvard-library-to-faculty-we.html

8   It is not our intention to underestimate the advances made by regional information and cataloguing systems such as SCIELO, REDALYC and Latindex in placing a large proportion of academic publications online. Our point is that they continue to depend on individual efforts, and also continue to face challenges in terms of discovery, standardisation and legal guarantees of circulation.

Working through public policy

Thanks to the new technological environment, humankind is moving ever closer to ensuring that everyone has the right "to share in scientific advancement and its benefits," as established in Article 27 of the Universal Declaration of Human Rights. However, achieving this goal requires efforts by national governments and the scientific community. In fact, the International Covenant on Economic, Social and Cultural Rights of 1996 obliges the states parties to the covenant to take steps "necessary for the conservation, the development and the diffusion of science and culture" and to recognise "the benefits to be derived from the encouragement and development of international contacts and co-operation in the scientific and cultural fields."[9]

The internet makes it possible to think about considerably expanding and guaranteeing mechanisms for the dissemination of scientific production as a means of enhancing the return on investments in science made by governments and institutions —and this return can be increased through open access models.

Governments can foster and develop various strategies in the framework of open access (the so-called gold and green routes) through the promotion of systems that guarantee mechanisms for the faster and wider sharing of the scientific knowledge produced with society as a whole. The implementation of the green route to open access would promote the creation of institutional repositories and networks of these repositories of scientific articles, which would entail the development of mechanisms for cataloguing, preservation and discovery, as well as eventual mechanisms for diffusion beyond the repositories. For its part, the gold route would foster the opening of journals,

---

9   See Article 15 in Officer of the High Commission for Human Rights (OHCHR). 1966. *International Covenant on Economic, Social and Cultural Rights* www.ohchr. org/EN/ProfessionalInterest/Pages/CESCR.aspx

new forms of sustainability for this means of dissemination, and the circulation of articles outside the journals themselves.

Finally, it would be especially useful to be able to modify the current models for the circulation of the findings of government-funded research,[10] for example, by following the strategies already successfully used in the policies of the European Union, the United States or even the World Bank.[11]

Now then, it would be particularly interesting to go even further and promote regional public policies at different levels so that open access dissemination processes also include collective strategies to give added value to systems for raising the visibility of scientific production, through the development of region indexes for the measurement of impact, quality, etc. If genuine regional leagues of scientific knowledge could be created, we would have more information of our own and more effective regional mechanisms to develop local policies than those derived from the current systems of private international monopolies. It is ambitious to promote a change like this, which would demand addressing the problem from various angles, but raising the issue could be the first step towards developing other paradigms in the sector.

---

10   Economic studies have shown that even small gestures aimed at increasing access to research findings can result in significant social and economic benefits. For example, according to a 2006 working paper by Houghton and Sheehan on the economic impact of enhanced access to research findings, "With the United States' GERD (gross domestic expenditure on research and development) at USD 312.5 billion and assuming social returns to R&D of 50%, a 5% in access and efficiency would have been worth USD 6 billion." www.cfses.com/documents/wp23.pdf

11   For more information on the open access initiatives mentioned here, see: European Union www.openaire.eu/es/open-access/mandates-a-policies, United States (NIH) www.publicaccess.nih.gov/policy.htm, World Bank www.live.worldbank.org/bank-open-access-policy-development-liveblog

Copyright laws and the creative economy: How can science and education in the digital age flourish in LAC?

Georgia Gibson-Henlin[1]

Science and education are concerned with the pursuit or transfer of knowledge. Both are always enhanced by access to information, persons and institutions, because this enables collaboration, which in turn increases and improves knowledge. The ability to create and access knowledge therefore seem to be key drivers for science and education to flourish in Latin America and the Caribbean (LAC).

From a legal perspective, the results of scientific research and educational material are subject to the rights of creators to determine who can use their works and under what conditions. Albeit for a limited period, these exclusive rights are protected by international treaties[2] and by national copyright laws, such as the Jamaican Copyright Act.[3] The justification for this restriction is that it enhances creativity. But at the same time there are legal exceptions to copyright laws that are intended to promote access to information at the most basic level, by permitting the transfer of knowledge, research and review and thus contributing to creativity in science and education.

---

1   Lawyer with over 10 years experience in digital intellectual property law, ICTs and internet governance. Attorney-at-law of the Jamaican and Ontario Bars.

2   Berne Convention on Copyright Law; World Copyright Treaty 1996 and World Performances and Phonograms Treaty 1996; Trade Related Aspects of Intellectual Property (TRIPS)

3   Jamaican Copyright Act (1993)

Nowadays it is accepted that the digital age and the creative economy provide many opportunities for improving knowledge and education. For example, the internet increasingly supports greater collaboration and interactivity. In addition, the infrastructure is built on the end-to-end principle and assumes access by everyone from anywhere –provided they have a device. However, copyright laws are often seen as inconsistent with the technological infrastructure of the digital economy.

At the same time, the web's underlying technology supports "freedom of access" and, ironically, this feature encourages creativity, in a manner similar to the restrictions afforded by copyright laws. This is because the technology enables all users –including copyright owners– to create or produce their content on the web. A unique feature of the digital age that benefits both users and rights holders is that the information can be "perfectly copied and instantaneously transmitted around the world".[4] In other words, rights holders' opportunities to profit from their work are not lost.

Exceptions to copyright law as a driver of creativity and education

The rights conferred by copyright laws to communicate the work to the public, to copy the work and to make adaptations of it exist in particular categories which have been the subject of international treaties and incorporated into local legislations.

Some exceptions to copyright laws drive creativity in science and education because they promote access to information in order to allow the transfer of knowledge, research and review. For example, "fair use" exceptions allow for research or private study and criticism or review of a protected work.[5] One of the

---

4   Sharpiro, Carl and Hal R. Varian. 1999. *Information Rules, A Strategic Guide to the Network Economy.* Harvard Business School Press. Harvard.

5   Ibid – S. 53

factors in determining fair use is "the purpose and character of the use".[6]

Access to copyrighted materials for education remains a contested area. An argument in favour of a flexible interpretation of an educational exception is that the cost of paying for the rights of each student to consult a work is an impediment to the delivery of education. This is especially true in places like the Caribbean, where the cost to purchase the rights for each individual would be prohibitive. Education and scientific research could benefit from lower costs of reproducing instructional and research material.

But the educational purpose restriction is certainly very narrow in terms of the Jamaican Copyright Act: "Copyright (...) is not infringed by its being copied in the course of instruction or preparation for instruction, provided the copying is done by a person giving or receiving instruction *and is not by means of a reprographic process*".[7]

In the digital age information is not copied by means of "reprographic copying". It is copied each time the information is refreshed, viewed, downloaded or shared. Thus, the internet has been described as "one giant, out-of-control copying machine".[8]

Rights holders reacted by creating what some would say is a new and greater impediment: they embedded digital rights management technologies in their works. These technological measures have received the protection of international treaties, which have already been incorporated into some domestic laws. Article 11 of the WIPO Copyright Treaty (1996), for example, requires contracting parties to implement legislation that provides effective legal remedies against "the circumvention

---

6   Ibid - S. 54

7   S. 56 [emphasis ours]. S. 2 defines "reprographic process" as "a process (a) for making facsimile copies; or (b) involving the use of an appliance for making multiple copies, and, in relation to work held in electronic form, includes any copying by electronic means."

8   Sharpiro, Carl et al., op. cit.

of effective technological measures that are used by authors in connection with the exercise of their rights." Article 12 of the same treaty requires the provision of legal remedies against persons who remove "electronic rights management information" or who distribute protected works knowing that electronic rights management information has been removed. Jamaica signed the treaty in 2002 but has not yet incorporated it into domestic law. In other jurisdictions, such as in the United States, the treaty provisions have been integrated into domestic legislation.

The Jamaican experience

Notwithstanding the limited exceptions in the treaties and legislation for instructional material at the most basic level, copyright laws do not appear to be the primary inhibitor to the growth and development of science in the digital age in Jamaica. The available data suggests that beyond secondary and tertiary level mainstream science degrees in medicine, there is little or no emphasis on research and development. There are few local research and development projects and little post-graduate or post-doctoral research in the sciences. In addition, the small number of local patent filings is highlighted as an indicator of limited work in the area of research and development in science and technology in Jamaica.

However, data obtained from the Jamaica Intellectual Property Office suggests that there is more local research and development than the patent filing figures suggest, because a large number come in for filing as "foreign" patents. This is mainly because of the unavailability of local investment support, which leads scientists to collaborate with overseas investment partners in order to complete the research and development and in some cases to exploit the patent. In Jamaica the major impediment to research is the lack of funding and investment support, not copyright regimes.

Strong institutional and governmental support:
The opportunities in the digital age

The apparent disincentives presented by restrictions on copying under copyright laws can also be alleviated through a top-down approach, by way of strong institutional and governmental support for the adoption and implementation of open and robust information and communications technology (ICT) policies.

The Jamaican government provides an example of strong governmental support for ICTs in education. It has instituted a robust e-government infrastructure which includes an education component. The e-Learning Jamaica Company Limited (e-LJam), an agency of the Ministry of Science, Technology, Energy and Mining, was formed in 2005. Its mandate is to provide support for incorporating ICTs in schools throughout Jamaica. In 2013, e-LJam signed a two-year lease with a United Kingdom-based entity to provide free online text books for students sitting their final secondary school exams. The e-LJam mandate also includes the provision of ICT hardware and software "as well as the development of digitised educational materials in eleven subjects to all high schools throughout the island".[9] However, one of the challenges to this programme is that access to the facilities is only available at school.

Another example of strong institutional support is provided by Professor Gordon Shirley, the principal of the University of the West Indies (UWI), Mona Campus. Shirley adopted the idea of his team to promote an e-book programme for the Faculty of Medical Sciences and has taken the bold move of launching the UWI Total Electronic Book Solution Tablet (TEST) during the 2013-2014 academic year to move that faculty to an e-learning platform. The programme will allow all medical students to have access to the core books that they require. This move

---

9   "Free online Textbooks for CXC Students" 13-03-2013 *Jamaica Observer* www.jamaicaobserver.com/NEWS/Free-online-textbook-for-CXC-students_13833562

will no doubt change the way that education is delivered at the Faculty of Medical Sciences and, in the near future, the entire University. The programme also allows for collaboration among the electronic libraries across all three UWI campuses.[10] This is a major plus because it spares students the significant costs of acquiring hard copy books. The only restriction, and it is a small price to pay, is that students should be careful to observe the copyright laws and notices embedded in the programme by the provider.

---

10   Trinidad, Barbados and Jamaica, including branch libraries on each campus.

Reflections on the digital world and the challenges ahead

Cosette Castro[1]

It is true that the digital world can open up good business opportunities, facilitate education and training, offer new jobs, and stimulate innovation and the development of new products, as well as new research involving the participation of numerous different fields. But this can only happen if and when there are clear and transparent public policies, developed in conjunction with academia, civil society and micro, small and medium-sized enterprises, and not merely with the support of big conglomerates in the communications, telecommunications or other sectors. When we think about public policies for the interactive digital content industries, and about the potential spaces for citizen participation in the digital world, we need to know more about the region with which we are dealing.

If public policies are not conceived as a space for social inclusion and sustainable development, they can lead to a deepening of the digital divide between those who have access and can effectively appropriate these new tools and knowledge, and the large majority of the region's inhabitants, who are not yet digitally literate, who use precarious technology like prepaid mobile phones and analogue radio and TV, and who are not in a position to pay for broadband (when the infrastructure exists in the country) or use the internet in general.

---

[1]   Professor and researcher in Universidade Católica de Brasília, Brazil. Coordinatos of the Working Group on Digital Contents for the Information Society, eLAC 2015.

Digital content refers to all audio, video, text or data material that circulates on tangible digital platforms or devices, such as mobile phones, computers, digital terrestrial television, digital radio, online videogames or digital cinema. This digital content circulating on tangible devices reaches millions of people by way of an intangible platform that exists only in the digital world: the internet.

In addition, this content (whether geared to information, entertainment, citizen expression or distance education and on whatever subject, from health to sports and culture) can circulate through different technological platforms at the same time, such as computers, mobile phones, open digital TV, digital radio, or online videogames, expanding on the notion that only computers –and more recently, mobile phones– can contribute to expanding access to information and social and digital inclusion in the region.

Users and producers of digital content in Latin America and the Caribbean

In Latin America and the Caribbean (LAC), we are still buyers of digital content, just as we are buyers of the technological platforms used to create or use digital content. Moreover, we buy access to the internet, a fragile network that is expensive throughout the region, since there are few regional policies aimed at offering, for example, free internet access for the population (urban or rural) in open or enclosed public spaces.

The materials created by content developers give rise to spaces for creation, production and circulation that go far beyond those intended by communications companies. This is because this content circulates through citizen participation (both individual and in organised movements) in the form of photos, videos, news stories, commentaries, jokes or parodies, moving in on the territory of the "institution" of the traditional media. Citizen journalism, a modern and virtual version of the popular and community-based communications of the 1970s and 1980s, seeks visibility through digital communications media, and shows us that another form of communication is possible, and can reach millions of people at a time, offering alternative views on the world.

The transition from the analogue to the digital world –a time which I have been metaphorically calling the "bridge phase" since 2008– can take place in different ways and be incorporated into society to different degrees, depending on the government's interest in approaching information and communications technologies (ICTs) as more than just technology per se. ICTs and the development of a digital content industry in the region could be geared to making people's lives easier through digital services, for example, with applications to set up doctor's appointments, pay taxes or use banking services, or for learning new skills and professional upgrading through distance education by way of free-to-air TV, online games or mobile phones, free of charge.

But no matter what public policies are proposed, in order for this transition to occur, it is also necessary for us as citizens to leave our "comfort zones" and observe our discourse and daily practices. This exercise in observation provides us with a surprising picture of how policy makers, public officials, politicians, artists, professors and researchers, among others, have adopted the discourse that the public is made up of mere users or consumers of digital technologies. By casting ourselves as "users" (who participate very little and are not at all proactive), many of us do not even realize that we produce digital content every day, even if it is just to comment on daily occurrences with family, friends or co-workers.

In contrast to the constant incitement to purchase and consume, the availability of digital content resulting from shared creation and free and open source software applications and services is expanded when access is greater and a larger number of different technological devices are used. The global movement that began with the collaborative creation of knowledge on the Wikipedia platform in the late 1990s is expanding through the growing possibilities for the use of applications and content under Creative Commons and copyleft licensing. It is also expanding due to the practices of the general public, through free music sharing, for example, and is growing with the circulation of movies, videos, series and new audiovisual narratives that circulate (even if only temporarily) thanks to audience participation. It is also taking on new dimensions, if we consider the collaborative or sharing economy and initiatives like crowdfunding.

Although most professors, intellectuals and journalists don't know it, in Brazil alone there are more than 30,000 pages by young writers who publish daily on websites and blogs, and an unknown number of independent producers of short videos for mobile phones, interactive storylines for videogames, series or short films for open digital TV or internet protocol TV, etc. In the meantime, there are a large number of educators, researchers, journalists and parents who, from their comfort zones, continue with the discourse of the linear and analogue world, often without being aware of the new situations.

They forget, ignore (or refuse to acknowledge) the 15,000 developers of free content, applications and services for open digital TV using Ginga middleware, and others who develop open-source software in LAC, providing solutions that can be used free of charge by the public, civil society organisations, universities, companies or governments. In addition to the lack of knowledge of these web-based collaborative creations, there is a continued belief that television is the villain, the cause of all our social ills. Yet we are a region of audiovisual culture, not printed culture, as our intellectuals and teachers would prefer.

While the intellectuals, professors, researchers and teachers in different areas continue with the discourse of how we could or should be, they miss the opportunity to take advantage of the obvious skills in the region for audiovisual and oral expression. These skills could be used to develop interactive public television, or take advantage of the potential for multiprogramming (the division of one channel into multiple sub-channels) to offer audiences a wider diversity of content.

Participation in social networks goes far beyond simple interpersonal interaction. For at least ten years, fans of TV series, soap operas, movies, comic strips or books have moved on to the creation of websites where they expand on the original stories. The Harry Potter series alone has inspired 21,000 pages of new storylines (or subplots) known as fan faction, or fanfic. For example, Harry's friend Hermione has acquired a family and siblings, not from the author of the original series, but through the creative work of fans. As well as expanding on the narratives around the main characters, fan fiction can also be used on various digital devices.

What does all of this mean? In addition to moving from the analogue world to the digital world, and being able to use different technological devices which, with the help of the internet, connect us to the rest of the world in seconds, we are also facing the challenge of moving from the role of consumers of digital content to that of producers of all kinds of content, in areas like journalism (informative content), entertainment, culture, distance education, sports, the environment, health, and so on.

We face the challenge of producing content for one or a number of public digital TV channels, for example, for government, educational, university, community or legislative channels. Another challenge is to offer new narrative experiences to the peoples of the LAC region, incorporating those which they themselves have developed.

What is needed is an ambitious project that must include:

- Interactivity, so that audiences can interact free of charge with television channels, using their remote controls.

- The portability and mobility of devices.
- Accessibility, so that audience members with different degrees of special needs can use digital technologies.
- The usability of devices for different population segments and levels of digital literacy.
- The interoperability of devices.
- The guarantee that services will be offered free of charge, to include all sectors of society.

Final considerations

One might think that once all these requirements have been met (and there is a big enough budget to deal with any pending issues), we will have everything ready. Unfortunately, this is not the case.

This is a much bigger project, which requires the participation of different sectors. In the case of broadband infrastructure, industry involvement is needed to produce TV sets and other devices that allow for interaction and media convergence, or to offer the public in the LAC region low-cost digital set-top boxes. This involves decisions that need to be jointly taken between governments and private companies, but should also include participation and monitoring by civil society.

There is also a need for public campaigns to raise awareness of the benefits of open and free digital TV and interactivity through the use of remote controls, or of how to upload content to TV channels. Incentives are also needed for media convergence.

At the same time, it is necessary to train the trainers –that is, to develop new university curricula that include digital subject areas beyond the use of computers. Professors and researchers need to catch up and leave behind the old discourse that "the government and big corporations are to blame." The time has come to play a more active role, to take on joint research projects between different provinces of the same country and different countries of the region.

This is a historic moment for the LAC region, and we need to know how many professors and researchers are studying the new possibilities for working on different technological platforms, to know more about the new professions in the digital world; how many are studying and experimenting with new narratives, transmedia and interactivity; how many are engaged in projects that integrate different fields (IT, information sciences, engineering, design, arts, education, etc.) And then this knowledge needs to be used as the basis for developing short-, medium- and long-term public policies.

5

PRIVACY

Is privacy dead? Proposals for a critical reflection on privacy protection in the age of internet

Claudio Ruiz[1]

The internet has changed the way we communicate, the way we interact, the way we access culture and information. To a large extent, it has changed the way we deal with the world. These changes, which are often good news (access, connectivity, immediacy), can also give rise to conflicts and problems from the perspective of rights. In particular, it is the traditional ways of understanding and approaching intellectual property rights and rights of privacy that are the most significantly affected by the new dynamics and practices arising from new information and communication technologies (ICTs).

In the case of privacy-related rights, the widespread use of ICTs has reopened old questions and raised new ones, primarily related to the treatment of people's personal information on these platforms. While it may have once seemed that privacy rights were covered by ensuring the right to be alone or to be free from state intrusion, the emergence of ICTs not only confronts us with old questions about the scope of privacy and "private life", but also with new ones concerning issues like consent for the processing of personal information by third parties. In fact, the terms which most commonly appear in the region's

---

[1] Executive director and founder of NGO Derechos Digitales in Santiago, Chile. He is also counselor of the Chilean National Council of Domain Names and IP numbers, and regional coordinator for Latin America of Creative Commons.

constitutions, to refer to the private versus public sphere, are "vida privada" (private life) or "intimidad", and some consider "privacidad" an unacceptable Anglicism.

In particular, the spread of so-called social networks is probably one of the most significant challenges to privacy in recent years. In the pre-digital age, there were a series of practices limited to the scope of the family unit or a close circle of trust, such as sharing memories or talking about social relationships. Social platforms have changed the way in which these practices are carried out, as personal messages are carried beyond the confines of traditional circles of trust and spread among groups with shared interests. As a result of these new practices, the line between public and private has become increasingly blurred.

In the meantime, regional and bilateral trade agreements have also implied a change in the way we address privacy from a regulatory point of view, especially with relation to the handling of personal data. LAC, in this regard, has been fertile ground for experimentation and the adaptation of foreign regulatory frameworks, whether through the adoption of European criteria or the acceptance of vaguer standards like those of the United States. Throughout the region, privacy tends to be a concept full of gaps, cracks and crevices that have been permeated by all manner of abuses and legislative laxity. The end result is an insufficient standard of protection and, even worse, a lack of reflection from within the region itself on the most problematic aspects of privacy in the 21st century.

Given the widespread use of these personal information practices, will privacy as we know it soon be a thing of the past? Do we need to abandon the idea of a right to private life, reformulate the concept, or perhaps devote ourselves to addressing the new risks that it faces? Should rights related to the processing of personal information by third parties be reconceptualised in the light of the paradigm shifts in new technologies? Has the time come to talk about new concepts and create new associations to know what needs to be protected? Or can existing international human rights instruments provide us with the leads and guidance we need for this critical analysis on privacy in the internet age?

Perhaps the leads towards answer to these questions are provided by the regulatory approaches to which Latin America has been exposed. Perhaps we can find other leads in local dynamics and practices and through reflection on these practices. If the concept of privacy as we once understood it is dead and gone, or must be reconceptualised, perhaps the starting point towards an answer can be found in these practices as well as in the way we have understood the concept in each country and in the region in the light of the development of basic rights.

Is privacy dead? Some reflections by way of an answer

Carlos Gregorio de Gràcia[1]

The first question that needs to be addressed is whether rights can die... and this is not an easy question to answer, at least from a legal point of view. Today we all believe that slavery (as in the right to own another person) is dead. And yet in Brazil, for example, cases of slave labour continue to be filed with the Tribunal Superior de Trabalho. On the other hand, when slavery was abolished in Brazil, a legislative decision was not considered sufficient: the minister of justice at the time, Rui Barbosa, ordered the burning of all written records of slave ownership, in the so-called Queima dos Arquivos da Escravidão.[2] This shows that rights do not only rely upon legal formalities, traditions or the administration of justice; other elements such as databases and other information sources play a significant role in their existence.

Therefore, in order to discuss the potential death of "privacy", we also need to ask how the right to privacy was born. Two different births can be defined. One took place in the United States, with the works of Warren and Brandeis in the 1890s,

---

1 Researcher and consultant with Instituto de Investigación para la Justicia, Uruguay

2 This incident (the burning of the slavery records), which took place in 1891, regardless of the controversy around its real motives, demonstrates that there is a close relationship between the "records" and rights, between the existence of the former and the validity of the latter, and that it not possible to guarantee certain rights if an active database is maintained, and vice versa. For this reason, it is not enough to look at privacy laws and their implementation; it is also necessary to analyse what personal information is recorded and for what purpose.

dealing primarily with the protection of one's private sexual life. The right to privacy per se is not addressed in the U.S. constitution, and has thus been shaped by the Supreme Court through a series of rulings, most of them handed down on cases related to sexuality, once again. To offer a recent example, a ruling in Vernonia School District v. Wayne Acton et ux. 515 U.S. 646 (1995) considers that athletes have a lesser expectation of privacy precisely due to the degree of public nudity entailed by their participation in sports (in communal locker rooms and showers, for example).

In the meantime, privacy was also born in Europe, but in this case, in the form of the protection of personal information. The underlying motive is a historical event: the extermination of Jews, Gypsies and other specific groups of people undertaken by the Nazis in Germany using census data to identify their victims. From this experience the Germans learned that the only way to protect citizens in the future, in the event of new concentrations of power, was to prevent the accumulation of personal information from the outset. This perception of the protection of personal information as a fundamental right spread throughout Europe.

It is therefore not surprising that the first Latin American law on the protection of information was adopted in Argentina in 1994 as a consequence of the inclusion of habeas data in a constitutional reform. Links could be drawn between the personal information protection movement in Argentina and the extermination practices of the military dictatorship (1976-1985). Not only did the military regime make use of the personal information gathered in the name of "state intelligence"; in addition, when individuals were captured, their telephone and address books were used to identify, investigate and capture the contacts listed in them.

From an information society perspective, the U.S. paradigm of privacy has lost relevance, because sexuality is no longer the taboo subject it was in 1890, and sexual issues are publicly addressed without a great deal of censure.

At the same time, the perception of the protection of personal information as a fundamental right as conceived by the European tradition is better suited to dealing with the problems of the information society. In the face of massive flows of sensitive information with no type of control or protection, the main risk that needs to be avoided is discrimination for unjust purposes.

This can be seen through a careful study of the most recent legislation on the privacy of health information in the United States,[3] which, we could say, has adopted the European paradigm of the protection of personal information and left far behind the concept of the right to be let alone of the traditional U.S. approach to privacy.

From the European perspective, the protection of information is one of the rights encompassed by the freedom of expression. This freedom includes first and foremost the right to express oneself, but it also includes the freedom of non-expression (also called informational self-determination, which is tantamount to the right to protection of personal information), as well as the freedom of audience. The implications of free speech can be addressed from either a "speaker-focused" or "audience-focused" perspective. The freedom of audience is concerned with offering citizens greater access to conflicting viewpoints and non-mainstream subject matter, not only because those with "disruptive" ideas have the right to be heard, but also because society has a special interest in hearing them. This updated view of the freedom of speech does not reinforce the right to express "eccentric" ideas, but rather places priority on the right of all citizens to have access to all ideas, and especially to those that do not coincide with their own way of thinking.

When we analyse current threats, it is evident that privacy and the protection of personal information are under attack, but they cannot die, because without these rights we would

---

3   See Privacy Act 5 U.S.C. § 552a, 45 CFR 160.103, Subpart E—Privacy of Individually Identifiable Health Information § 164.501 and in particular HITECH Act TITLE XIII- Subtitle D—Privacy - SEC. 13400

be much more vulnerable to discrimination (in access to employment, credit, insurance, health care, etc.) with no means of protection.

In the context of the current development of the information society, a number of rights are critically endangered. First of all, the right to anonymity and anonymous speech, since the enormous amount of data in circulation has given rise to the emergence of mathematical algorithms that can be used to "de-anonymise" data. Studies on databases of medical prescriptions have found that the probability of de-anonymising patient data based on a postal code and date of birth is 69%, and if the patient is over 60 years of age, that probability rises to 95%.[4]

Freedom of speech is also endangered. While it may be possible to express oneself more freely, it is difficult to access differing opinions, because the tendency is to follow known figures, while the views of unknown figures remain relatively inaccessible. In this regard, the so-called Google filter bubble infringes on the freedom of speech from an audience-focused perspective: search results are presented according to criteria based on previous searches, which means that alternative viewpoints may be left out.

The protection of personal information is also at risk, not necessarily due to technological developments, but rather as the result of legal decisions in both Europe and the Americas, where the classification of data as protected or unprotected is justified on the basis of a "predominant public interest". In 2001, the Privacy Commissioner of Canada determined that the name of a physician on a medical prescription does not qualify as protected personal information. In a similar vein, the U.S. Supreme Court ruled that free access to the names of physicians is justified by legitimate corporate interests.[5] These decisions

---

4   Sweeney, L. 1997. "Weaving Technology and Policy Together to Maintain Confidentiality". *Journal of Law, Medicine & Ethics, 25*, nos. *2&3*: 98-110 www.dataprivacylab.org/dataprivacy/projects/law/jlme.pdf

5   Sorrell v. IMS Health Inc., 23 June 2011

served to expand the already established concept of public figures –and their consequent loss of privacy– to partially public figures, a category which could be extrapolated to include all professionals in the exercise of their professions.

In Latin America, the right to the protection of personal information has followed the European route in Argentina, Uruguay, Mexico, Peru, Colombia and Costa Rica. In other countries, laws are still evolving. Agencies for the protection of personal data in the region are still very weak. In Argentina, for example, only 25 fines have been imposed during the more than 12 years that the law has been in force, while in Spain there can be this many fines in a single day. Ironically, the adoption of data protection laws in the Latin American region was motivated more by the desire to tap into the call centre market[6] than to ensure respect for a fundamental right (with the possible exception of Mexico and Colombia).[7]

While attacks on personal information can come from both the state and from private companies, those from companies are more dangerous. Some would argue against this statement, primarily because states handle sensitive information on their citizens. However, there is a qualitative difference, namely the existence of laws on access to public information. In Latin America –with the exception of Argentina– and particularly in Mexico, access to information laws pre-dated data protection laws, and have provided citizens with the opportunity to know what information is in the state's possession. Consider, for

---

6   There are studies that link the expansion of the call centre market in Argentina to its certification by the European Commission as providing an "adequate level of protection" for personal information (Decision 2003/490/CE). Since the operations of offshore call centres (for example, when calls made by users in Europe are forwarded to customer service agents in Argentina) involve the handling of personal information, a declaration of equivalent legislation would provide users with a guarantee of the protection of that information.

7   Remolina, Nelson. 2013. "41 personas condenadas por el delito de violación de datos personales y 544 multas por infracción de la ley 1266 de 2008" 18-04-13 *Observatorio Ciro Angarita Barón* www.habeasdatacolombia.uniandes.edu.co/?p=980

example, the destruction of the RENAUT (National Registry of Mobile Telephony Users) database in Mexico, ordered by the Federal Institute for Access to Information and Data Protection to protect the privacy of mobile users.[8] Paradoxically, since 2003 there has been a law in force in Argentina establishing free access to environmental information which includes private companies.[9] In many cases, people are unaware of how much information on them is in the possession of companies, and how and for what purposes that information is being used. If there is no authority responsible for guaranteeing the protection of personal information, and if exemplary financial penalties are not imposed, it is unlikely that any company will change its policies.

Ultimately, the protection of privacy and personal information is not dead, but it does need to be revitalised. This will require efforts to raise awareness among citizens regarding how necessary these rights are for their daily lives, and among the authorities regarding respect for human rights and the rule of law.

---

8   "Destruye Segob bases de datos personales del Renaut" 15-06-2012 *Proceso* www.proceso.com.mx/?p=311021

9   República Argentina. *Ley 25.831 Régimen de libre acceso a la información pública ambiental.* www.infoleg.gob.ar/infolegInternet/anexos/90000-94999/91548/norma.htm

Online Spying in Latin America

Katitza Rodriguez[1]

The explosion of online expression we've seen in the past decade is now being followed by an explosion of communications surveillance. Technologies can also open a Pandora's box of previously unimaginable state surveillance intrusions. For instance, the Internet and mobile telephony are no longer platforms where private communication is shielded from governments knowing when, where, and with whom a communication has occurred. The capacity of new technologies to instantly aggregate and analyze data makes it a beacon of one's online presence. The Electronic Frontier Foundation (EFF)[2] believes that "metadata"–information logging individuals' communication activities– is as sensitive as the content of communication and therefore deserves stronger human rights protections.

This is why, at the end of 2012, EFF organized a workshop,[3] where a mix of experts, journalists, lawyers and activists from around the world, particularly from Latin America mapped specific problems posed by invasive surveillance infrastructure, and government access to peoples' data. More than anything

---

1   International Rights Director of the Electronic Frontier Foundation (EFF).

2   A non for profit membership organization fighting for people's rights on the internet and working hard to keep the internet open and free. Founded in 1990, it has one simple goal: to ensure that everyone's rights would be respected in the online world.

3   State Surveillance and Human Rights Camp wiki.surveillancehumanrights.org/ Electronic_Surveillance_And_Human_Rights_Camp

else, what one learned was the critical role that context – the unique political histories and conflicts, socio-cultural expectations, and surrounding foreign and national policies– plays in shaping how state surveillance programs and practices are being carried out. This includes who and what can be surveilled and the ability of citizens to challenge surveillance. In spite of these disparate conditions, some surveillance practices are common to Latin America and continue to reappear amidst very different contexts.

Surveillance in context

While most Latin American countries have democratically-elected governments, few have traditions of strong privacy protections. Intense political instability, internal wars, and military regimes have long established cultures of state surveillance in many countries.[4] Colombia, Peru, Mexico, Paraguay, and other Central Americans countries have experienced multiple internal wars: the war against terrorism and the war against drug trafficking to name a few. These wars have created a reactionary climate and have bred a rapid expansion of surveillance architecture.

On the other side of the spectrum, countries like Argentina and Chile have endured military regimes but have not faced similarly intensive drug wars and terrorism conflicts. Nevertheless, many such countries, including Argentina, have instituted compulsory national ID schemes and have stored the information in huge databases. Those databases, which are themselves remnants of previous military regimes, are currently being "modernized" to collect biometric identifiers in several countries in the region. In Colombia and Peru, surveillance technologies have been repurposed to silence judges and

---

4   Surveillance and Human Rights *EFF* www.eff.org/issues/surveillance-human-rights

opposition voices,[5] demonstrating the ease with which they can be abused to subvert the rule of law in any democratic nation lacking robust checks and balances.

Distinct contexts for those with access to technology

Why does a government chooses to surveil its citizens? What legal limitations and safeguards have been established? Are these enforced? How do citizens react and perceive state surveillance? The answers to these questions, of course, depend on context. The realities of individual countries vary drastically. The problem can be divided into distinct contexts for those with access to technology and for those on the other side of the digital divide. Activists and people in urban settings (bloggers, journalists at large, news companies, online activists) and those working in rural areas (indigenous activists, environmental activists, rural and community journalists) have noted differences in surveillance practices, tactics, and problems –particularly in areas where conflicts around mining and large-scale resource extraction are taking place. Many of the most violent conflicts in Peru, Mexico, and Central America are occurring in rural areas often in the context of the war on drugs. The added attention intensifies surveillance mainly due to the added foreign aid.

Role of the United States in surveillance technologies in Latin America

For several years, the US Drug Enforcement Agency (DEA) has been providing cooperation to Latin American States to fortify local law enforcement and intelligence agency efforts to

---

5   "The Politics of Surveillance: The Erosion of Privacy in Latin America" Katitza Rodriguez 22-07-11 *EFF* www.eff.org/deeplinks/2011/07/politics-surveillance-erosion-privacy-latin-america

combat drug trafficking. This aid in surveillance technology has been implicated in abuses of power. For instance, the Colombian government illegally spied on political opponents and human rights activists rather than on drug lords.[6] The "Las Chuzadas" scandal erupted around former Colombian President Alvaro Uribe and Colombia's intelligence agency[7] privacy abuses in 2009. As a result, a former head of the intelligence agency from 2002-2005, Jorge Noguera, was sentenced to 25 years in jail for illegally spying on political activists and collaborating with paramilitary death squads.

Leaked US diplomatic cables shed light on the DEA's communications surveillance program.[8] In the cases of Paraguay and Panama, the US government was pressured to permit the use of these technologies to spy on leftist groups in operations unrelated to narcotics investigations.

Major challenges in Latin America

Challenging the assumption that surveillance equals security

In many regional contexts, civilians have embraced new security measures under the misconception that more intrusive measures will naturally lead to greater security. In countries like Guatemala, civil society groups have even advocated for laws opposing basic privacy protections,[9] such a law requiring mobile phones to be registered. In Mexico, various groups

---

6   "U.S. aid implicated in abuses of power in Colombia" Karen DeYoung y Claudia J. Duque. 20-08-11 *The Washington Post* www.washingtonpost.com/national/national-security/us-aid-implicated-in-abuses-of-power-in-colombia/2011/06/21/gIQABrZpSJ_story.html

7   Departamento Administrativo de Seguridad - DAS

8   See note 3.

9   "Organizaciones piden norma para registro de celulares" 12-01-12 *PrensaLibre. com* www.prensalibre.com/noticias/Piden-norma-registro-celulares_0_626337376. html

strongly supported[10] a geolocalization bill that allows authorities to track location data without a warrant.[11] Attendees of EFF Surveillance and Human Rights Camp[12] noted that all too often the public does not challenge the government and private sector surveillance that is taking place and many simply accept these activities without question.

Law enforcement approaching service providers without legally-required authorization

A growing concern is the number of law enforcement officers skirting the law by asking service providers to simply fork over information without any sort of search warrant. Even when legal procedures, such as a search warrant, exist, police increasingly request information without obtaining a legal authorization. Nevertheless, they often expect full compliance from service providers.

Chile

In 2008, a Chilean website called Huelga.cl ("strike" in English) was approached by the Cyber Crime Section of the Chilean Police. The site is an online space for coordinating union actions. The agency demanded that the webmaster hand over data related to pseudonymous user accounts, such as IP addresses, records of previous connections, real names, and physical addresses. The targeted users had left comments on a website about an ongoing strike.

In this case, because police did not have a court order to back up the request for information, Huelga.cl took a stand by

---

10   "Ley de Geolocalización" 28-03-12 *Mexico SOS* mexicosos.org/news/ley-de-geolocalización

11   "La 'ley de Geolocalización' permitirá 'rastrear' a usuarios de celular" Leonardo Peralta 27-03-12 CNN México mexico.cnn.com/tecnologia/2012/03/27/la-ley-de-geolocalizacion-permitira-rastrear-a-usuarios-de-celular

12   See note 3.

resisting police pressure and refusing to hand over the data without a fight. For legal assistance, they turned to Derechos Digitales (Digital Rights), a Chilean online human rights nonprofit organization, and managed to resist the request.

In another case, the Regional Director of the Chilean Department of Labor, the agency responsible for ensuring the enforcement of labor laws, sent a letter to Huelga.cl simply demanding the removal of "inappropriate content" from their website along with the disclosure of user information[13], but it was only for administrative purposes as opposed to serious criminal investigations. Huegal.cl again refused to comply and instead, made the director's demands public.[14]

It is not always the case that service providers can resist extralegal government requests, find legal advice or have enough economic resources to fight against those demands as Huelga.cl did. Huelga.cl should be praised for speaking up and managing to make the request from law enforcement public.

Governments pressure private sector

Governments frequently impose heavy fines for non-compliance with their requests for data access. This form of coercion acts as a mechanism of enforcement over service providers and can raise serious concerns for free expression. The service provider is left with little incentive or option to resist illegitimate requests from the government when they are threatened with heavy fines.

---

13 "Respuesta a Director Nacional de Trabajo" 17-09-10 www.derechosdigitales. org/wp-content/uploads/Respuesta-a-DT.pdf

14 "Huelga.cl resiste presión de Dirección del Trabajo por entregar información de usuarios" 20-09-10 www.derechosdigitales.org/2010/09/20/huelga-cl-resiste-presion-de-direccion-del-trabajo-por-entregar-informacion-de-usuarios/

Brazil

In 2012, a judge from northern Brazil froze Google's accounts and imposed a fine on the company for refusing to remove three anonymous blogs or reveal contact details of the bloggers.[15]

The content of the blogs stated the mayor of Varzea Alegre of corruption and embezzlement.[16]

While some companies might be able to withstand governmental pressure, alarms were raised that this won't be the case for smaller companies that lack resources and influence. This is particularly true in contexts where heavy fines for noncompliance are written into legislation, and companies are not given legal avenues to appeal or fight the fine.

Foreign governments access to individuals' data in the cloud

Governments are increasingly seeking to negotiate access or interception capabilities to user data with companies that do not lie within their jurisdictions. This form of access is complicated because it is not always clear which country's laws apply or to what extent. Because of the complex nature of these requests, governments often look for "easy" solutions that call for voluntary disclosure of information or simply allow full access to the user data.

While the internet is technically borderless, in reality, state actors impose their sovereignty onto online environments with increasing frequency. The exercise of sovereignty[17] over shared spaces can subject individuals to the laws of another country

---

15   "Juiz determina bloqueio de R$ 225 mil da Google" 19-08-11 Diário do Nordeste diariodonordeste.globo.com/materia.asp?codigo=1028611

16   "Google fined in Brazil for refusing to reveal bloggers' identities" Anna Heim 20-08-11 *The Next Web* thenextweb.com/la/2011/08/20/google-fined-in-brazil-for-refusing-to-reveal-bloggers-identities/

17   "Cloudy Jurisdiction: Addressing the thirst for Cloud Data in Domestic Legal Processes" Internet Governance Forum - Baku 2012 www.eff.org/document/cloudy-jurisdiction-addressing-thirst-cloud-data-domestic-legal-processes

without any awareness on their part that this has happened. This in effect transforms the surveillance efforts of one country into privacy risks for all the world's citizens. There have been none public debate about this topic in Latin America.

The need for international due process

States are faced daily with the challenge of protecting their populations from potential and real threats. To detect and respond to them, many governments surveil communication networks, physical movements, and transactional records. Though surveillance by its nature compromises individual privacy, and hence, can be used only in exceptional situations where state surveillance is justified. Yet, if state surveillance is unnecessary or overreaching, with weak legal safeguards and a failure to follow due process, it can become disproportionate to the threat –infringing on people's privacy rights.

This is why EFF and a group of NGOs including ADC in Argentina, Privacy International and Access Now have developed a set of International Principles on the Application of Human Rights to Communications Surveillance.[18] We attempt to explain how the law that already exists should be applied in the current digital environment, particularly in light of the increase in and changes to communications surveillance technologies and techniques. These principles are the outcome of a global consultation with civil society groups, industry and international experts in communications surveillance law, policy and technology.

Conclusion

Context plays a critical role in shaping how state surveillance programs and practices are handled. While many differences

---

18   This set of principles can be found at necessaryandproportionate.org

exist, some surveillance practices are common throughout the region. U.S. foreign aid for surveillance, while intended to combat crime, has been used for practices that lead to abuse.

State agencies and law enforcement are increasingly outsourcing investigations to private companies who are not under the same sort of judicial oversight as official law enforcement entities would be. The increasingly close and non-transparent connection between the private sector and law enforcement needs to be addressed, as it poses a risk to the rights and freedoms of the individual. Of major concern is the notion that private companies are routinely complying with the requests of law enforcement in the absence of due process. We encourage further research and documentation of this phenomenon.

At a time when efforts by states to conduct communications surveillance are rapidly proliferating across the globe, there is a need to remind States of their international human rights obligations. The aforementioned set of International Principles on the Application of Human Rights to Communications Surveillance should attemp to explain how the law that already exists should be applied in the current digital environment, particularly in light of the increase in and changes to communications surveillance technologies and techniques.

Privacy and the exaggerated reports of its death

Ramiro Álvarez[1]

"If you don't have anything to hide, you don't have anything to fear". "Privacy is essentially a bourgeois Western construct. It is a right that needs to be limited for the pursuit of legitimate ends". "There is no reason to be worried over the shrinking of private spaces in a democracy". "Our own practices as internet citizens lead to greater transparency around everything we do, and that's a good thing". "It's preferable to give up a bit of our privacy if it makes us feel safer: *The more we know about ourselves, the better we can take care of ourselves*".

These are some of the arguments put forward in public debate on issues involving our right to privacy, for example, when the observation is made that the internet blurs the lines between private and public life. Some of these arguments are powerful because they appeal to emotional factors or use other strategies to be more convincing. Some make concrete promises in response to supposedly hypothetical fears. In any event, they are all mistaken.

The right to privacy was one of the first to be recognised constitutionally. The idea that the state cannot interfere with our private correspondence, enter our homes or seize our personal documents without a court order emerged as a reaction of early liberal constitutionalism to the abuses of monarchical absolutism. And protection of this right has always been

---

1   Director of the Information Access Area at Civil Rights Association (Asociación por los Derechos Civiles - ADC), Argentina.

perceived as something fundamental: without a space protected from the view of others, full political participation is impossible, because our freedom of communication and association would be curtailed. From this perspective, "*Privacy* is not something that I'm merely entitled to, it's an absolute prerequisite".

This Marlon Brando quote captures a key aspect of the discussion, because it presents a powerful argument which nonetheless is very difficult to get across: that democracy and our freedoms need room to breathe. Creativity, irreverence and the questioning of authority cannot flourish if we are permanently under watch. These spaces of freedom are crucial, and this is what gives us the right to challenge any policies and practices that serve to make them smaller and harder to come by.

In recent years, these spaces free from the view of others have shrunk enormously for two basic reasons. The first relates to the technological advances that have made it increasingly easier, cheaper and more efficient to implement mass surveillance and social control policies. Security cameras are rapidly multiplying, every move we make is recorded by credit card transactions and the customer "loyalty" programmes of the businesses we patronise, and our mobile phones make it very easy for a complete stranger to know where we are at any given moment. The second reason is that we have adopted much riskier practices: all of our personal information is in the cloud, we buy and sell goods and services over the internet, and we announce to the whole world when we are going on vacation, where we are and what we are eating.

This shrinking of private spaces sometimes comes hand in hand with the promise of concrete benefits.

We experienced an example of this when the national government of Argentina decided to create a unified public transit fare system, known as SUBE.[2] The SUBE card was the

---

2   Unified Electronic Fare System (SUBE).

sensation of the summer of 2012. Long queues of citizens, with their national ID cards in hand, eagerly lined up to register with a system that promised to be much more efficient, that would let us use all the different means of public transportation without having to scrape together the coins needed to pay the exact fare. But for some reason, the system included the recording of all of our movements, which were entered into a database every time we used public transit. Why did the state want this information?

We were told that the information was valuable, for example, for an assessment of how citizens use public transport. But did they want to know how many people were travelling and how, or who was travelling? Moreover, the system offered no protection of personal information whatsoever: simply by knowing the card number, anyone could access the travel itinerary of the cardholder over the internet. If I lost my wallet and my SUBE card was in it, for example, anyone who found it would be able to determine where I live, approximately where I work, and what time I leave home and come back every day.

The most powerful argument, however, was that the card would make it possible to create a differentiated system of subsidies for electronic fares: using this data, and assessing the income situation of each citizen, the government could determine whether or not they deserved to have their daily travel through the city subsidised by the government. To make matters worse, we were not informed that it was possible to register for a SUBE card anonymously, which meant most people presented their ID documents when applying even though it wasn't actually necessary.

A much more dangerous move, which went largely unnoticed in Argentina, was the launching of the Federal System of Biometric Identification for Security (SIBIOS), a database that gathers biometric data from the country's citizens. For the moment, it is limited to fingerprints and photographs. In the future, however, the information stored will include our iris configurations and DNA, at least if we are to believe the

Orwellian video produced by the government to present the system, which additionally informs us that the technology used was developed in collaboration with... Cuba.[3]

What is most striking about the video –in addition to a certain aesthetic similarity to the Michael Radford film *1984*, based on Orwell's novel and released in 1984– is the shameless way it promises concrete benefits in terms of security. The video tells us how these new technologies will serve to fight crime, how human trafficking will be almost impossible once the system is fully operating, and how the system of security cameras could –soon– identify all of us, in order to determine where we are at all times. Because, the more we know about ourselves, the better we can take care of ourselves.

It is important to remember how policies like these were justified to the public. With SUBE, we were promised efficiency and convenience. With SIBIOS, greater security. In exchange, the state asked us to limit our private space a little bit more. After all, what do we have to fear from a democratic government? Could the authorities possibly be interested in what time I leave my house? Could a massive gathering and recording of personal data possibly become –once again– a key component of a plan to kidnap and "disappear" citizens?

The right to privacy is not dead, but it is suffering from an extremely poor state of health, because the defence of this right constantly comes up against these kinds of arguments. And it ends up losing, because the dangers of the policies that are gradually encroaching on the right to privacy are perceived as hypothetical, theoretical. The benefits, on the other hand, are concrete and verifiable: the convenience of SUBE, the sense of greater security provided by security cameras, etcetera, etcetera.

---

3   The video is available at: www.youtube.com/watch?v=QjrRNExTCx8. The argument highlighted in the first paragraph –*the more we know about ourselves, the better we can take care of ourselves*– is a slogan used by the government to sell the system.

This means that those of us who believe that the right to privacy is fundamental in a democracy have our work cut out for us. We need to take the ethical and political arguments in favour of the defence of a personal space protected from the view of others and present them in a convincing way. Ethical arguments are perhaps not the most efficient these days. But I would not be willing to give them up for even a second. Nevertheless, these arguments need to be complemented by additional arguments, such as those that question the objectives of these policies, their effectiveness and their feasibility; those that question the discriminatory practices that these policies could be used to support; those that focus on the secondary impacts; and so on.

Much of this discussion should in fact revolve around the promises that have been made. Are biometric identification systems actually infallible? Not only are they not infallible, but they are also rife with problems and technological flaws that make them useless for doing what they promise to do. Is it actually possible to identify people captured on security cameras based on their facial features? Today, it isn't. But even if it were possible, do we really want to live in a society like that? What would we be giving up in exchange for this hypothetical security they are offering us?

Efforts to maintain significant spaces of privacy will need to appeal to these arguments, and other better ones. Challenging the encroachment on our fundamental rights will require more research and innovative ways to share the results of that research. We will also need to pick our battles intelligently. And here in the 21st century, in the midst of the new technologies that hold us in their thrall, it will be no small task to revindicate the political principles of early constitutionalism, which wisely told us –and tell us– that freedom needs room to breathe. And that without privacy, no freedom is possible.

The Lives of Others

Beatriz Busaniche[1]

East Berlin, 1984. The Stasi, East Germany's secret police, keep the country's citizens under constant surveillance. Stasi officer Gerd Wiesler, alias HGWXX/7, devotes hours of every work day to spying on a well-known playwright and loyal supporter of the Communist regime. A Stasi team plants bugs throughout the playwright's apartment and sets up surveillance equipment in the building's basement. The surveillance has nothing to do with the playwright's loyalty to the regime or lack thereof; the real reason behind it is the fact that Minister of Culture covets the playwright's girlfriend, a beautiful woman who gives into the government official's advances because to do otherwise would threaten her career as an actress.

The prize-winning German film *Das Leben der Anderen* (The Lives of Others), directed by Florian Henckel, depicts a society under constant watch, and an all-powerful state that arbitrarily intrudes in the lives of the citizens of the former East Germany. It portrays an outdated model of state surveillance, the targeted surveillance of individuals typical of the 20th century and the Cold War, a model of surveillance that involved significant resources, entire teams of personnel specifically devoted to this task and the necessary technical support, and the identification

---

1   Fundación Vía Libre. Graduate in Social Communication, Public Leader of Creative Commons in Argentina, member and founder of Wikimedia Argentina, and lecturer at Universidad de Buenos Aires.

of individuals to be monitored on the basis of some particular reason: their opinions, political activities, or, as in the case depicted in the film, some aspect of their personal lives. A team of spies watching every move a person makes from a certain moment forward. Our societies have changed, and so have our models of surveillance.

Personal surveillance vs. mass monitoring

Our world is overrun with devices designed for the detection, surveillance and monitoring of people. But it is no longer a matter of personally spying on certain selected individuals, as in the film mentioned above, but rather a socio-technical system with the capacity to track and record almost all of our movements, our preferences, our thoughts. The drastic rise in technology-mediated monitoring is, without a doubt, a defining characteristic of our era.

Personal surveillance continues to exist, targeted to previously identified individuals on the basis of some particular suspicion or interest. In general, it is legally used to fight crime and terrorism. Of course, it is also used illegally to monitor government opponents, journalists, judges or other individuals with the aim of influencing their decisions or taking some type of action against them (kidnapping, robbery, etc.).

In a democratic society, the use of personal surveillance by the state is supposed to be mediated by the exercise of due process in order to safeguard basic rights, which means each act of personal surveillance should be backed by at least a court order. The history of democratic countries demonstrates that the right to privacy is generally recognised in national constitutions that expressly prohibit state intrusion into the homes, personal records, correspondence and lives in general of individuals, without the proper legal guarantees and permissions.

However, it is difficult to discuss mass monitoring in these terms, since in many cases it involves the use of systems installed in public areas, where the objects of surveillance have not been previously identified. These systems are reminiscent of the dystopian novels of the 20th century such as George Orwell's *1984*. Even when every citizen knows that she or he is being observed through the eye of a camera, it is difficult for people to fully grasp what this means as long as no action is specifically taken against them as a result, nor can they know exactly what is being observed by the observer.

Mass monitoring is sometimes the specific purpose of a certain technology. In other cases, it is an indirect consequence of systems designed to offer other types of service. One of the most common examples of the former is the surveillance of public and private spaces through video systems; the latter include mobile telephony, which can be used to establish the physical location of the users of the service (see textbox at the end). All of these systems, whether designed for the purpose of surveillance or not, form part of a new model of mass surveillance that some researchers have come to refer to as dataveillance.[2]

Connected/monitored

The possibilities for the collection of personal data have increased in large part due to the growing extent to which we live our lives online. The invaluable opportunities opened up by digital technologies and internet access for communication, interaction, organisation, learning, reading, visiting faraway places, shopping, and an endless list of other activities, entail a direct trade-off in terms of privacy.

2   See Clarke, Roger. 1988. "Information Technology and Dataveillance" *Association for Computing Machinery* www.rogerclarke.com/DV/CACM88.html

Anonymity on the web is an endangered species. The systems that we use leave a trail of traceable digital footprints with every online activity in which we engage: surfing websites, sending email, participating in social network platforms, downloading various types of content. People who wish to maintain their anonymity must take deliberate steps. Identifiable tracks like the IP addresses we use to connect to the internet, user authentication for session initiation and so-called cookies are part of countless applications that we use every day, and the gathering of this data goes practically unnoticed. As if this were not enough, we are also witnessing a growing trend in the requirement of personal identification for the use of various services, particularly social networks. The collection of personal data during online activity is ongoing, widespread and increasingly unnoticed by users who tend to have little in-depth knowledge of the applications they use, or who use them without even reading the terms of use. Every time we click "like" on a website we are contributing to the creation of our online profile.

Collection/processing

This massive collection of data would useless without the technical conditions for its processing. It is not simply a matter of capturing images or gathering millions and millions of pieces of personal data, but rather of building systems that can give meaning to this data for those who will eventually use it. The storage and processing capacity of these systems has increased exponentially, and major improvements have been developed for the organisation and recovery of vast amounts of data. Today information can be easily compressed and moved, categorised and managed, interpreted like never before, making it more valuable, reliable and efficient. These innovative tools enable new forms of control and use of personal data and information.[3]

---

3   Nissenbaum, Helen. 2010. *Privacy in Context: Technology, Policy, and the Integrity of Social Life*. Stanford University Press. Palo Alto, CA.

Social networking platforms offer prime examples in terms of the collection and processing of personal data, with Facebook accounting for some of the most high-profile incidents. There are a number of troubling phenomena involved here, beginning with what people post about themselves without considering the consequences of their behaviour. The media have reported countless cases of people being fired from their jobs, divorces and various other personal problems resulting from information posted by the people affected themselves. A second concern relates to the information posted by other parties, including photographs, anecdotes and comments that infringe on the private lives of individuals without their permission. Also problematic is the widespread practice of giving the companies that provide social networking services access to the email addresses of our contacts in order to send invitations and build up our online community.

But the most complex problem arising from social networks is not merely related to the posting and storage of personal data, but rather the patterns that emerge from the interactions between the people connected there. These provide information that can be used to develop profiles based group membership, opinions and consumption habits which can be used for various purposes, from targeted advertising and market studies to the monitoring and control of political and activist groups.

State/private sector

As we have seen so far, the issue of surveillance and threats to privacy has numerous different facets. One element we have considered is the role of the state and the growing implementation of mass monitoring systems, such as surveillance equipment in public areas, or systems for the validation of the identity and control of individuals. Examples range from the installation of CCTV cameras in different municipalities to the creation of centralised databases of biometric information from the entire population (such as the SIBIOS system in Argentina).[4] In this regard, not only is the state encroaching on the individual rights of citizens in a context of significant asymmetry of power, but its conduct also contributes to narrowing the possibility for citizens to turn to the state for the guarantee and defence of their rights.

A second element of concern is the ever growing and increasingly widespread collection of data by private sector actors. These include financial service companies (banks, credit card companies) and internet service companies (Facebook, Twitter, Google, Microsoft, etc.) which offer free services that are ever more widely used. The privacy policies of these companies tend to be overlooked by users who are generally not well versed in analysing legal terms of use, added to which is the additional challenge of dealing with regulations established beyond national borders.

A third troubling aspect involves the social practices that actively encourage individuals to engage in public exposure. Not only do we expose our own private lives, but we also form part of the multidimensional intrusion into the private lives of others.

In all three cases, however, the central characteristic is asymmetry, in terms of both the collection of information and our ability to control the handling and use of our personal data.

We are being watched. Whether we like it or not, this is the defining feature of our era. Are we willing to give up our privacy?

---

4   Federal System of Biometric Identification for Security (SIBIOS)

Direct monitoring takes place through the installation of systems expressly devoted to this purpose, for example, video surveillance systems in public and private spaces. Different justifications, such as fighting terrorism or protecting citizens from crime, have resulted in the proliferation of closed circuit television (CCTV) systems for the monitoring of public areas in various cities. Parks, streets, bus terminals, airports, areas around public buildings, even entire neighbourhoods are continuously monitored by the systems, which capture images that can be viewed in real time or recorded and stored for viewing at a later time. People in cities like Buenos Aires are monitored and captured on camera dozens of times in a single day.[a] In London, statistics show that a person moving around the city will be caught on CCTV cameras an average of 300 times a day.[b] The equipment used has become increasingly cheaper as well as increasingly advanced through the incorporation of more and better technology. The continuous monitoring of public spaces by public authorities is complemented by private monitoring initiatives involving the installation of video surveillance systems in apartment and office buildings by private security companies. There has been a striking increase in sales of these systems and services, for reasons such as the protection of older adults who live alone or of young children in the care of non-family members (in nursery schools, day care centres and even in private homes where children are watched by babysitters or nannies).

Indirect monitoring takes place as a consequence of the use of technologies designed for other purposes, such as navigating one's way around a city (GPS systems) or telecommunications (mobile telephony systems). In these and other cases, the gathering of data results from the original design of the system, although it is not the primary purpose. This category also includes, for example, payment with credit cards, which leaves a permanent record of our movements; the use of electronic key cards to enter certain places (office buildings, universities, etc.); electronic prepaid public transit systems (such as the SUBE card in Argentina)[c] or prepaid toll systems on highways; and telephone bills that include details of calls and their duration, or mobile telephony systems that need to track our geographical location in order to provide us with service.

---

a A map of the location of surveillance cameras in public areas in the city of Buenos Aires is available at www.camaras.buenosaires.gob.ar/

b Rosen, Jeffrey. 2004. The Naked Crowd: Reclaiming Security and Freedom in an Anxious Age. New York. Random House

c Unified Electronic Fare System (SUBE).

6

CONNECTING THE PAST AND THE FUTURE

ICT for development milestones and approaches in Latin America and the Caribbean

Valeria Betancourt[1]

At a conceptual level, there is universal agreement regarding the potential offered by information and communications technologies (ICTs) for promoting human development and economic growth. At a practical level, most governments in Latin America and the Caribbean (LAC) have formulated digital agendas and adopted other public policy measures aimed at the incorporation of ICT access and usage in different areas of development. ICT-enabled strategies have also been developed to foster new forms of citizen participation and contribute to the modernisation of public management and public service provision. Nevertheless, more than a decade after the first discussions around this theme in LAC, and despite the significant progress made in the creation of regional and national agendas, ICT access and use for the purposes of development remain key challenges for the region.

It would be useful to take a look back at the past in order to determine how best to move forward in the future.

---

1   Coordinator of the Communications and Information Policy Program for Latin America (CIPP-LA) of the Association for Progressive Communications (APC) and a consultant for the project 25 years of the Information Society in Latin America & the Caribbean.

Evolution

According to figures provided by Richard Heeks in a paper on ICT and development, in 1998 less than one out of every 100 inhabitants was an internet user and two out of every 100 inhabitants were mobile phone subscribers in developing countries, including the countries of the LAC region.[2] Recent estimates from the International Telecommunication Union (2013) indicate that today, 31 out of every 100 inhabitants in developing countries are internet users, while the mobile-cellular penetration rate in these countries is now 89%.[3] How has this leap in ICT usage rates between the late 1990s and 2013 been manifested in the region? Have the explosion in mobile telephony penetration and growth in internet users translated into significant progress in the achievement of development goals in LAC? Have development obstacles related to ICT access and use in the region been reduced or eliminated?

It is undeniable that the advances in access to and use of ICTs, particularly the internet, have transformed the economic, social, cultural and political life of the countries of the region, and the ICT for development agenda has obviously become more complex and diverse in the last decade. In addition, there are a series of issues that constantly emerge and will be relevant for the regional ICT for development agenda in the next ten years, one of which is internet governance.[4]

---

2   Heeks, R. 2010. "Development 2.0: Transformative ICT-Enabled Development Models and Impacts". *Short paper n° 11*. University of Manchester, Centre for Development Informatics. www.sed.manchester.ac.uk/idpm/research/publications/wp/di/#sp

3   ITU. 2013. "The World in 2013. ICT facts and figures". www.itu.int/net/pressoffice/press_releases/2013/05.aspx#.UTkTFhjgORs

4   The Working Group on Internet Governance, set up by the Secretary-General of the United Nations in December 2003 in accordance with the mandate given to him during the first phase of the World Summit on the Information Society (WSIS), agreed on the following working definition: "Internet governance is the development and application by Governments, the private sector and civil society, in their respective roles, of shared principles, norms, rules, decision-making procedures,

It is worth reviewing some of the most important milestones in the evolution of the ICT for development agenda and policies in LAC.

The first initiatives involving internet connectivity for the purposes of development were undertaken in the early 1980s by progressive organisations, academics and universities as a way to expand the possibilities for communication and action by civil society in the region. While there were already cases of commercial and public internet use at the time, it is these initiatives that represent the origins of the use of computer networks for social change and development.

This is not a minor detail. It is no coincidence that, in the midst of a militarised world, it was organisations committed to peace, human rights and the environment who promoted advances in the interconnection of social movements, academics, activist groups and civil society organisations through electronic communications. The way in which civil society and academia began to connect with "new" technologies in the region set the precedent for placing these technologies at the service of development goals.

The years 1995 and 1996 marked the beginning of the large-scale availability of internet and mobile phone service in LAC. This led to the need for governments to respond, through public policies, to the expansion of ICT access and use, as a means of pursuing insertion in the information society and providing effective solutions for the so-called digital divide.

However, it wasn't until July 2000 that the governments of the region, convened by ECLAC and the Government of Brazil,

---

and programmes that shape the evolution and use of the Internet." It should be noted that the Working Group specifically stressed that internet governance is not limited to internet names and addresses, but also includes other critical internet resources and developmental issues pertaining to the use of the internet, such as access, among others. See Working Group on Internet Governance. 2005. Report of the Working Group on Internet Governance. Château de Bossey. www.itu.int/wsis/wgig/docs/wgig-report.pdf

signed the Florianópolis Declaration, which focused specifically on the use of ICTs for development. It would be safe to say that, at the governmental level, this declaration marked the beginning of the formulation of strategies and policies aimed at capitalising on the potential of ICTs for promoting economic growth and social development. The declaration expressed "the shared aspirations of the Latin American and Caribbean countries to become full-fledged members of the information society by the year 2005 on an efficient, effective and sustainable basis within the framework of the global knowledge-based economy."[5]

ECLAC reports: "As part of the international process of the World Summit on the Information Society (WSIS), which took place in two phases (Genève in 2003 and Tunis in 2005), the region's authorities intensified their efforts to create a regional perspective on the development of information societies. Various meetings held between 2001 and 2003 by the regional network of the United Nations' Working Group on ICTs emphasized the importance of collaboration between stakeholders interested in confronting this challenge. Moreover, the Agenda for Connectivity in the Americas and the Quito Plan of Action (August 2002) insisted on the need to design realistic national strategies and action plans."[6]

This political dialogue –and the resulting commitment– among the governments of the region were reflected, to a greater extent, in the Bávaro Declaration[7] (2003), which established the fundamental principles for building information and knowledge societies in the region and gave rise, in 2005, to the formulation of the Plan of Action for the Information Society in Latin

---

5   CEPAL. 2000. "Declaración de Florianópolis". www.eclac.org/publicaciones/xml/2/4312/florianopolis.htm

6   CEPAL. 2010. "Consulta pública: ¿qué dicen los expertos sobre eLAC 2010-2015?" www.eclac.org/cgi-bin/getprod.asp?xml=/elac2015/noticias/paginas/2/44102/P44102.xml&xsl=/elac2015/tpl/p18f.xsl&base=/elac2015/tpl/top-bottom.xsl

7   CEPAL 2003 "Declaración de Bávaro". www.eclac.cl/prensa/noticias/noticias/9/11719/Bavarofinalesp.pdf

America and the Caribbean, commonly referred to as eLAC. The first plan of action established concrete targets for 2007 based on the commitment made by the region's countries to adopt a set of national public policies, together with regionally coordinated measures aimed at accelerating and strengthening the building of information societies. In this regard, eLAC offered strategic orientation and guiding principles for the development of ICT policies in the region in areas such as access and digital inclusion, capacity building and knowledge creation, public transparency and efficiency, instruments to enhance the coordination of digital development policies, and actions to foster an enabling environment for digital development.

Various civil society actors from LAC became actively and substantially involved in the WSIS process to contribute to forging an understanding of the social, cultural, economic and political impacts of the use of ICTs, particularly the internet, and to offer approaches and solutions for the development of democratic, inclusive and equitable information societies. Civil society actors from the region contributed to placing a number of issues on the discussion table related to the right to communication (revisiting and resignifying the debates and proposals of the New World Information and Communication Order), the convergence of the information and communications industries, the deepening of structural divides (including the digital divide), internet governance, and regulatory and policy frameworks. Their views and proposals are gathered in the civil society declaration "Shaping Information Societies for Human Needs".[8] This involvement extended to the regional eLAC process as well. Civil society was instrumental in ensuring the participation of non-governmental stakeholders (including the private sector and technical community) in the eLAC coordination mechanism. Civil society, the technical community and the private sector currently occupy formal roles as observers in eLAC.

---

8   Civil Society – World Summit on the Information Society. 2003. "Declaración final". www.itu.int/wsis/docs/geneva/civil-society-declaration-es.pdf

Ten years after WSIS, determining whether the region has made progress in the crystallisation of the principles stated and the implementation of the agreements adopted for the development of information and knowledge societies remains a valid question.

The Association for Progressive Communications (APC) is conducting a critical review of the changes that have taken place since the adoption of the WSIS Declaration of Principles and Plan of Action in 2003. The evidence gathered suggests that globally, eradication of poverty, for example, has not been a high priority in policy discussions and agendas related to information and knowledge societies, and the Millennium Development Goals have played an insignificant role in ICT decision- and policy-making processes at the national level. The evidence further suggests that both the WSIS Declaration of Principles and the civil society declaration on WSIS have had very little influence on the formulation of ICT for development agendas and policies.

The impact of the relationship between ICT and development therefore remains an open question in the region.

Key themes in the beginning: Concepts, policy and practice

The emergence of specific agendas on ICT for development in the region essentially came about as a response to various agreements adopted by governments from the year 2000 onwards. These agendas emerged on an isolated basis, and in most cases were not shaped by an integrated vision and long-term policy decisions at the national level.9 Instead they have

---

9   The creation of digital agendas to frame information society policies and pro-grammes is quite recent in Latin America. Ten countries of the region currently have national-level digital agendas: Argentina, Brazil, Chile, Colombia, Costa Rica, Ecuador, Mexico, Paraguay, Peru and Uruguay. The English-speaking countries of the Caribbean have created a joint system for "Monitoring Caribbean Information Societies" to support ICT action plans and initiatives. The region's first digital agen-

arisen as projects or initiatives aimed specifically at such objectives as the rollout of ICT infrastructure, improvement of education, modernisation of public management and administration, support for agricultural development, boosting productivity, and others. Initiatives for the incorporation of ICTs to improve public health care services probably constitute the area that has most lagged behind.

In the meantime, there have been efforts undertaken by non-governmental organisations to implement ICT projects that address a variety of development issues, including the provision of public access to the internet. In many cases, governmental and non-governmental projects and initiatives have been launched with financial support from development and cooperation agencies in Europe and North America, as well as various United Nations agencies.

The countries of the region have not followed a single model of ICT access, use and appropriation. Nevertheless, two conceptual and practical approaches for tapping the potential of ICTs to promote social development and economic growth have predominated: the strengthening of the ICT sector (based on the production of ICT goods and services) and the implementation of ICTs in specific areas of development. While the dilemma of whether it is more effective to prioritise one approach or the other (development of ICTs vs. development with ICTs) has not been fully resolved at the conceptual level, in practical terms, different countries have adopted different emphases and to different degrees. A number have chosen to combine the two approaches, based on the understanding that ICT access, use and appropriation take place in the structural framework of Latin American societies and respond to the economic, social, cultural and political dynamics of those societies. The particular approach adopted has in turn determined the logic guiding the formulation of public policies.

---

da was launched in Chile in 2007, but the rest of the countries generally began implementation of their digital agendas between 2010 and 2011.

The guiding logic of ICT policy making has not been consistent throughout the countries of the region, either. Policy decisions have been shaped by the views and interests of the policy makers of the day, configurations of power, the availability or lack of evidence on the issue in question, and other factors. "Lack of transparency and political will, bureaucratic inertia, low levels of public understanding of and interest in policy issues, and counter arguments promoted by interests with their own agendas in mind"[10] have further complicated ICT for development policy making in the countries of the region.

In several of its numerous studies on the development of the information society in LAC, ECLAC notes that the predominant technological paradigm has been exogenous to the region, resulting in slow and uneven development from the centre to the periphery and extending existing structural gaps to the digital sphere.

An analysis of the concrete experience of the implementation of ICTs in specific areas of development in the countries of the region can shed light on whether governments have primarily adopted a passive stance, or whether they have worked "to stimulate the accumulation of new technological and organisational capabilities and to have some successes in harnessing ICT applications to development goals".[11]

While tangible and visible advances have been made in the majority of countries, ICT policy development in the region has been unequal, and a great deal still needs to be done to move beyond political agreements when it comes to regional cooperation for the implementation of projects and the adoption of harmonised regulation.

---

10   Bruce Girard and E. Acosta y Lara (eds.) 2012. *Impact 2.0: New mechanisms for linking research and policy*. Fundación Comunica, Montevideo.

11   Mansell, Robin. 1999. "Information and communication technologies for development: assesing the potential and the risks". *Telecommunications Policy 1999 Vol. 23,1*.

Connecting ICT4D experience in LAC to the new open development environment

Manuel Acevedo[1]

1. Characteristics of open development

In order to explore the open development environment in Latin American and the Caribbean (LAC), it is useful to identify linkages between advances in ICT for development (ICT4D) and the characteristics of open development. On the basis of a study conducted as part of the project 25 Years of the Information Society in LAC, this article considers the ways in which these ICT4D advances could pave the way towards the emergence of open development schemes and strategies, as well as identifying some specific challenges that the region poses for the integration of "openness" in its development agenda.

We should start with an interpretation of the concept of open development. According to Smith, Elder and Emdon, "Open development refers to an emerging set of possibilities to catalyze positive change through 'open' information-networked activities in international development".[2] They also specify that what is important is "openness that serves the purpose of development, not openness for openness' sake". In a related

---

1   External evaluator of the program Institute for Connectivity in the Americas of the IDRC and a consultant for the project 25 years of the Information Society in Latin America & the Caribbean.

2   Smith, Matthew L.; Laurent Elder and Heloise Emdon. 2011. "Open Development: A New Theory for ICT4D". *ITID (7:1), Spring 2011, iii–ix.*

paper, Smith and Elder write about open social arrangements enabled by ICTs that are characterised by expanded access and increased participation, which in turn facilitate more collaborative production modes.

To simplify, we could say that open development refers to development processes that enable more people to participate and exercise their agency for positive change, through better access to information and related tools (particularly ICTs) as well as more collaborative approaches via networked processes/structures. Thus, one way to determine the present stage and potential for open development would be to examine the progress made on these three specific factors through the ICT4D agenda/work in LAC since approximately the year 2000.

1.1 Access

Among the range of resources that need to be accessed for an open development process, two that are related to ICT4D activities are fundamental: ICTs and information resources. Since 2000, the region as a whole has advanced significantly on both fronts.

Latin America and the Caribbean is the developing region with the highest levels of internet access. The percentage of the region's population that have used the internet reached 43% in mid-2012, although there are marked differences between countries (Chile and Uruguay stood at slightly over 50%, as compared to Nicaragua and Guatemala at just over 10%).[3] The rapid expansion of mobile internet through smartphones could mean continued rapid growth of internet access during the remainder of the decade.

By information resources, we refer to relevant data, information and knowledge. A number of international organisations like the World Bank have opened up their data

---

3   Miniwatts Marketing Group. Internet World Stats www.internetworldstats. com/stats.htm

to the world, and this includes relevant data for LAC. Many countries in the region, including the most influential ones (Brazil, Mexico, Argentina, Colombia, Chile, Venezuela), have adopted commitments as part of the Open Government Partnership. New organisations like the Observatory for the Information Society in LAC (OSILAC) have helped create a body of solid statistical data on the availability and use of ICTs at the national level,[4] which is particularly valuable for policy making. Significant volumes of information on any developmental area are now accessible, although the level of content production in the region in the predominant languages (Spanish, Portuguese) is still modest as compared to content in English (the lingua franca for substantive development information), except in a few selected areas like governance or education.

In terms of knowledge, we focus on research and knowledge management practices. The amount of research about ICT4D and the information society in the region has increased substantially since 2000, when it was essentially non-existent. Organisations like ECLAC,[5] DIRSI[6] and OSILAC have either carried out solid research or helped other organisations to do so. Some thematic areas present more advanced research, such as infrastructure (regulatory frameworks, access prices, etc.) or education. However, the extent of research is still relatively small in most thematic areas (health, economy, environment, natural disasters, etc.) and there are few entities that carry out information society-related research.

1.2 Participation

Participation is a desired characteristic of democratic governance. It goes beyond the political arena when we adopt a wider meaning of governance, as put forth by the Spanish sociologist Joan Prats: "the

---

4   OSILAC. ICT Estadistical Information System www.eclac.cl/tic/flash/
5   Economic Commission for Latin America and the Caribbean (ECLAC).
6   Regional Dialogue for the Information Society in LAC.

capacity of a society to confront its challenges".[7] Both individual and organisational participation related to development and ICTs have increased in Latin American and the Caribbean – the first as a consequence of emerging e-government and digital democracy practices, such as the pioneering participatory budget initiative in Porto Alegre (Brazil), extended later to many other municipalities in the region; and the second as observed in sectoral participation in processes that build the basis for the information society. An analysis of individual participation is more difficult to cover in a short space, so we will concentrate here on organisational or stakeholder participation.

The World Summit for the Information Society (WSIS) stimulated the emergence of "multi-stakeholderism" in the region when dealing with these topics. During the preparatory phase leading to the first WSIS conference (Geneva, December 2003), civil society organisations across the region started to come together to work on priority issues as well as reaching out to government delegations from their own countries. The same occurred with the private sector, albeit on a more modest scale, with the Ibero-American Association of Research Centers and Telecommunications Companies (AHCIET) centralising private sector representation. WSIS dealt with too many issues, and governments in the region with limited capacity benefited from the technical knowledge of NGOs and academics in the sector. Countries like Uruguay even included individuals from outside government in their official delegations. While the official WSIS processes still kept NGOs out of decision making, there was routine contact and collaboration among the different stakeholders, who even joined together formally in instances like the Working Group on Internet Governance (WGIG), which was created in the interim between the two phases

---

7   Prats i Català, Joan. 2002. "Gobernabilidad democrática en América Latina fini-secular (Instituciones, gobiernos, liderazgos)". *Paper No. 2, Colección de papers*. Instituto Internacional de Gobernabilidad, Barcelona, España. www.iigov.org/papers/tema1/paper0002.htm

(December 2003-November 2005) and later led to the present Internet Governance Forum (IGF).

The eLAC process continued with this partial multi-stakeholder orientation, though without significant advances from the situation in 2003 and 2005. eLAC is an intergovernmental process, where other types of organisations participate but without official status. There is a monitoring committee with non-governmental actors as observers, for instance, and many of the contributions from civil society occur in the thematic committees (e.g. on education) via government officials. Formal multi-stakeholder processes with influence and responsibility over decision making (agreements, policies, commitments, etc.) have yet to be implemented. Nationally, there is more direct civil society involvement in policy making, such as the public consultations in Ecuador while drafting the new constitution in 2008, or during the preparation of the first Digital Agenda in Argentina in 2009.

There are other regional forums with active multi-stakeholder profiles. The LAC IGF is where civil society is most active and represented, although its recommendations (like those of the global IGF) are not binding. At the operational level, the more flexible and inclusive thematic networks (e.g. Red GeALC[8] on governance and the eSAC[9] project network on health) have enabled various stakeholders to work together directly, and have in fact become multi-stakeholder platforms supporting important advances in terms of both policy and practice.

1.3 Collaboration

Some academics and practitioners prefer the concept of "network society" proposed by Castells to the more ambiguous

---

8   Network of e-Government Leaders of Latin America and the Caribbean (Red-GeALC)

9   Public eHealth Innovation and Equity in Latin America and the Caribbean (eSAC)

concepts of "information society" or "knowledge societies". In any case, networks constitute a differentiating factor in the way social and productive structures are organised today, because of the large number of them and the high degree of efficacy that some of them attain.

Networks are appropriate environments for carrying out development programmes and activities because of a number of factors that include (i) their flexibility, (ii) their inclusive tendencies (which facilitate participation), (iii) the ease of sharing information and knowledge, and (iv) geographical ranges that can extend beyond the national scope. But what is perhaps more important, and integrates all of the above, is their potential to foster and channel collaborative work for development, which is at the core of the idea of open development.

LAC has seen a flourishing of development networks since 2000, aided as in other regions by greater ICT access and the emergence of simple and powerful communication tools (web 2.0), but with possibly two distinguishing characteristics. One is the linguistic effect, with the vast majority of the population speaking either Spanish or Portuguese, including a growing share of people who can understand both (given their similarities). The second characteristic is cultural, and refers to a predisposition for human, personal communications.

Some of the most successful development initiatives in LAC related to the information society have been implemented through networks or using networking practices. Networks like RELPE[10] or Educared in education, GeALC in e-government, DIRSI or ACORN-REDECOM[11] in academic ICT4D research, RICG[12] in public procurement, the vocational training institute

---

10   Latin American Network of Educational Portals (RELPE).

11   Americas Communication Research Network (ACORN-REDECOM).

12   Interamerican Network of Government Procurement.

network at CINTEFOR,[13] CLARA[14] in science and technology research, APC in the area of communication rights, etc., have made and continue to make significant contributions in their fields. Networking practices, meanwhile, are at the operational core of major initiatives like the eLAC process, the creation of a regional eHealth Agenda and the intercountry coordination on the management of electronic waste.

However, there are challenges in terms of the sustainability and stability of most development networks in LAC, which need to be confronted if network activities are to serve as the operational basis of open development work in the region.

2. Challenges for open development in Latin America and the Caribbean

There are many potential areas for open development that provide opportunities for the people of LAC, but they do not yet show a clear and "open" path. Some of these fields relate to internet governance, intellectual property, collaborative business models, digital citizenship and privacy, and were debated at the colloquium Open Development: Exploring the future of the information society in LAC (Montevideo, April 2013).

In terms of the three above-mentioned factors of access, participation and collaboration, the research carried out in the 25 Years project suggests some specific challenges to deal with over the next few years. If successfully addressed, the outcomes could strengthen the operational framework of open development in LAC in the medium and long term, and could even begin to generate effects in the short term.

---

13   Interamerican Center for the Development of Knowledge in Vocational Training.
14   Latin American Advanced Networks Cooperation.

2.1 Access

LAC has the highest internet penetration among developing regions, but it is about half that of OECD countries (nearing 80%). Besides the wide differences among countries, the share of broadband internet subscriptions (fixed plus mobile) is only about 30% of total internet access.[15] The new broadband strategies being discussed for LAC need to go beyond faster and wider connectivity. More importantly, they should incorporate an integrated agenda for access that explicitly and decidedly addresses capacity (building) and demand (generation). This entails, in essence, crafting a kind of "broadband governance" that can enable open development that reaches beyond those who already enjoy access.

In terms of access to knowledge, there is a need to increase both the quantity and the quality of research in LAC on information society issues.[16] Few national organisations (such as universities) or international development organisations (IDRC, EU and APC are notable exceptions) actively foster or conduct ICT4D or information society research. There are no academic journals or specialised periodic publications in LAC about ICT4D or information society issues. The eLAC process, successful in other aspects of its work, never put in motion a research agenda.

In particular, there is still limited analysis/research on what open development can mean for LAC; on the adaptation of the dynamics of ICT-mediated sharing, cooperation, participation and collaboration in various regional contexts (context is

---

15 ITU Telecommunications Database 2012, in Katz & Galperin 2013. Katz, R.L.; Galperin, H. 2013. "La brecha de demanda: determinantes y políticas públicas" IN Jordán, V.; Galperín, H; Peres, W. eds. *Banda ancha en América Latina: más allá de la conectividad*. UN Economic Commission for Latin America and the Caribbean (ECLAC). Santiago de Chile.

16 An aspect that is not covered here for lack of space, and which is important, is that governments in the region should comply with the growing number of open data and open access policies, which often only exist on paper, as it continues to be difficult for citizens or organisations to actually access the public data to which they should be entitled by law.

everything in development); on whether and how an agenda for open development could emerge; etc.

2.2 Participation

What does multi-stakeholderism mean in open development processes? While multi-stakeholder participation in information society issues has taken off since 2000, there is a need to consolidate it in practice for effective and influential open development interventions to take place. This possibly implies introducing non-governmental sectors into some aspects of decision making (such as open data policies/practices) as well as the assumption of responsibilities. It has not happened yet at the regional level (eLAC) or uniformly at the national level.

Increasing and extending participation does not necessarily mean reducing the role of the state. One of the political trends in LAC since 2000 has been precisely the "return of the state" from an earlier weakening phase marked by the Washington Consensus (which now elicits consensus in the region only with regard to its failures and limitations). Open development strategies need to consider how to strengthen the state "just enough" to facilitate effective multi-stakeholder participation, for instance, through effective e-governance platforms and strategies.

A different kind of multi-stakeholder process is observed within the domain of civil society itself. In most LAC countries the relatively small number of CSOs specialising in ICT4D or the information society concentrate on policy issues and devote most of their efforts to attempting to interact with governments and other stakeholders. A consequence is that they dedicate comparatively little effort to working with other CSOs in thematic areas (agriculture, education, gender, etc.) in order to strengthen their ICT capacity. This is a pattern that it would be beneficial to reverse in order to more effectively involve the entire civil society sector in open development processes.

2.3 Collaboration

Open development is almost by definition a networked approach to development. But is the current state of most development networks adequate for widespread, productive collaboration? Most development networks today do not have network-specific strategies, management or analysis. Little is known about composite network effects (i.e. when changes in a network component may affect other components). Collaborative work in development networks seems to be more of an art than a science, and the application of methodologies such as social network analysis (SNA) is rare. As Martin Hilbert observed in an interview conducted for the 25 Years project, in relation to networks and development work, "We know the nodes, but not the networks."

Perhaps the region is presently at an early, "network 1.0" stage, and needs to evolve towards more standardised and rational "network 2.0" stages, which take advantage of the positive attributes of networks in terms of flexibility, inclusiveness and creativity to improve their productivity (as is the case, for example, with open source software production). This will require a fresh understanding by development agencies (national and international) of ways to provide preferred support for networks (however compact or decentralised) –an approach strongly favoured by IDRC, and few others. This would include activities for institutional network strengthening, including proper indicators and monitoring methods, to move in the direction of "results-based networks".[17]

These challenges of low productivity, instability and financial unsustainability found today in LAC need to be overcome in order for development networks to serve as the key implementers of open development processes.

---

17   In line with the common development practices of "results-based" management, indicators, programming, etc.

3. Some final reflections on open development in LAC

From the perspective of emerging open development processes in LAC, this article has argued that:

(i) In relation to access to ICTs, the balance is relatively positive, with new broadband strategies that can substantially diminish digital divides; while with regard to access to knowledge, the extent of research on information society issues is insufficient.

(ii) In terms of participation, the advances in multi-stakeholder work (more in projects/activities, less in processes) have been significant but could be further consolidated into effective contributions to decision making.

(iii) Regarding collaboration, many development-oriented networks have emerged and made important developmental contributions; however, they tend to be unsustainable and do not utilise network-tailored organisational methodologies.

Thus the overall picture is one of relatively positive readiness for open development in LAC, which would be increased if some relatively affordable challenges are met. Such challenges (increasing research, improving network performance, etc.) cannot be met in the short term, but could possibly yield gradual, noticeable effects over the medium and longer term.

Finally, we suggest a few additional points that straddle across these factors and can also contribute to more effective open development work:

• *Re-examining the convenience of institutional strengthening as a development instrument.* Today, donor support goes almost exclusively to "action" (or targeted) projects. There are hardly any initiatives that seek organisational strengthening as an explicit objective (particularly among NGOs). A new development approach like open development may require fresh new institutional support to ensure it is demand-driven.

- *ICT mainstreaming.* The knowledge gained in specific ICT4D work by development actors (including governments) is often only partially absorbed by other units or initiatives due to institutional inertia. Specific policies may be needed to accelerate changes to fully integrate the use of ICTs across organisational departments, ministries, etc.

- *Research-to-policy bridging.* It is not easy to connect research to policy processes, so specific attention to the dynamics involved (including projects or activities specifically aimed at improving these connections, such as the Impact 2.0 project[18] by Fundación Comunica and IDRC) may be in order. For the innovative approaches espoused by open development, awareness building for policy makers will be particularly needed.

- *Monitoring and evaluation.* This is one of the "laggard" areas in ICT4D work. Knowledge about proper indicators and methodologies is scarce, and the capacity/expertise to use that knowledge is even scarcer. Open development processes should invest in generating the necessary knowledge and capacity, as part of institutional strengthening (internally and in the field).

---

18   Girard, Bruce and E. Acosta y Lara (eds.) 2012. *Impact 2.0: New mechanisms for linking research and policy.* Fundación Comunica. Montevideo.

CONCLUSION

Openness and Development[1]

Robin Mansell, Fernando Perini and Bruce Girard[2]

The term *open development* is gaining traction as a way of focusing attention on a number of tensions that exist in the pursuit of economic and social development in a society increasingly dependent on information. While acknowledging that access to technology remains an important problem, more and more, the key question is not *whether* societies will take advantage of the spread of digital technologies, networks and applications, but *how* they will do it. *Open development* highlights that our information society is characterized by a number of contending forces calling for different levels of openness.

On the one hand, certain sectors put greater priority into an approach characterized by stronger control of information, communication and networks, focusing on secure information exchange, information scarcity safeguarded through copyright, and rapid, market-led technological platforms driving innovation and economic growth. On the other hand, are the sectors that promote open approaches fostering commons-led information sharing, access to knowledge, and bottom up and decentralized collaborative and generative innovation. Both approaches have very different answers to policy and practice, creating tensions that need to be constantly addressed as the information society emerges in Latin America and the Caribbean.

---

1   These conclusions build on the report of the debates held during the second day of the seminar Open Development: Exploring the future of the information society in Latin America and the Caribbean held in Montevideo on April 2013.

2   Bruce Girard is Director of Fundación Comunica.

If our preference is in line with the goals of inclusive and equitable development that ensures respect for human rights, freedom of expression and the right to a reasonable degree of privacy, then there is a key role for policy makers, the private sector and civil society to ensure that the balance that is struck favours those goals. While certain controls over networks and content may be desirable, they should not create or reinforce inequalities. A more inclusive development requires a balance between contending approaches.

Our path towards an inclusive information society in Latin America and the Caribbean is by no means guaranteed. The various expert perspectives presented in this book show that there are several important challenges to building more equitable and inclusive information or knowledge societies. The following summarizes some of the priorities that emerged from the debates around the different topics during the Open Development meeting in Montevideo and highlighted in this book and can serve as guide to policy and practice in the region's emerging information society.

There is a need to defend the principles of an open internet in Latin America and the Caribbean, which are increasingly under threat.

The experts gathered in Montevideo agreed that it is fundamental to defend the openness principles that guided the development of the internet against a growing number of threats, including:

- Legislative reforms and state interventions in areas such as cybercrime and copyright that exert excessive control over content and may curtail human rights, including the rights to freedom of expression and association.
- Invasive practices in the management of network infrastructure (by operators and/or intermediaries) that threaten privacy, and lead to economic and social discrimination and persecution.

- For some users, closed and limited access services may be more attractive than paying for access to all available services and information. Eventually this user behavior can intensify the concentration in a few closed systems and "walled gardens" that limit users' access to the open internet.

Governments should embrace the opportunities for new forms of digital citizenship while considering whether they are consistent with fully participatory democratic practice.

Despite initiatives to incorporate technology into government and the delivery of services, it is important to recognize that the wide variety of potential interactive models between society and the State are not yet reflected adequately in the practice of governance in the region. If we want new forms of digital participation to contribute to consolidating and improving democratic governance in the region, it is important to acknowledge that:

- Governments must strive to be more transparent and open to participation. This will require significant changes in the vision of the State itself as well as the development of new capabilities.

- It is important to monitor whether States are developing interactive platforms that enable effective engagement with citizens and incorporate their voices into government decisions.

- New forms of digital citizenship must be consistent with and responsive to the history of traditional social movements, which have always incorporated collective action as a central component.

- There is a fundamental need to build citizens' capacity to participate effectively in the new interactive platforms. Otherwise, the voices which are heard online will reflect and reinforce traditional inequalities in our societies.

Previously excluded sectors are beginning to collaborate in a range of online platforms that challenge established formal structures and enable alternative pathways for development.

New models that build on the capacity of voluntary or informal coordination in online communities are beginning to reach groups that previously were excluded from the global economy and to have an impact in their lives. People are increasingly using the internet to share time, resources, skills, money and many other key resources and assets in innovative ways, creating new ways to offer more affordable products and services with greater environmental sustainability. It is fundamental to understand how these new forms of sharing are filling gaps and meeting citizen needs, complementing or disrupting the formal economy and public services alike.

- A growing number of platforms is expanding the capacity of online and offline communities to create solutions for their aspirations, including by improving access to basic needs such as health, income and education.

- Increasingly, these new collaborative models are becoming more important to the base of the pyramid. It is important to map and document effective bottom-up strategies in order to devise better ways to harness their potential for tackling pressing social needs.

- There is a need to understand the spectrum of online interaction that is taking place beyond the market in order to explore emerging forms of social innovation. At the same time, as they became widespread, it is important to understand how they need to be regulated.

The contribution of copyright to the increasingly digital creative economy is becoming increasingly contentious in our societies. Nevertheless, there are many opportunities to develop balanced approaches.

Our societies are facing a growing polarization among supporters and skeptics in relation to the role of copyright in the digital economy. On the one hand, there is a growing pressure to strengthen these protections and their enforcement, for example, by requiring them as part of international trade agreements. On the other hand, those in favour of more collaborative economic and social arrangements tend to focus on eventual distortions in relation to wider access to and appropriation of knowledge enabled by information technologies. Acknowledging that this is likely to remain a contested issue, a number of recommendations highlight some of the areas where we should target our efforts:

- Gather specific cases to demonstrate the concrete impact of existing intellectual property rights legislation on local and regional contexts, their eventual distortions to access to knowledge, and the implications for social and economic arrangements.

- Explore public policies that can stimulate open licensing of academic, scientific, governmental, and cultural production, as a way to stimulate social and economic development and to reduce critical gaps in access to knowledge in the region.

- Call for more transparent and multi-sectoral processes for international negotiations that involve potential changes in intellectual property regimes.

- Connect the regulation of intellectual property rights with human rights so there is a balance between fundamental rights (freedom of expression and access to information) and the interests of the creative industry in copyright enforcement.

- Expand the concept of innovation beyond market-driven technological processes, acknowledging the contribution of shared and collaborative knowledge arrangements to the sustainability of different social and economic activities and to greater equity in the society.

Privacy is facing significant threats in the region increasingly connected by technology. There is increasing evidence that shows that without decisive action, new forms of social and economic discrimination will expand.

Privacy is a concept undergoing substantial change in societies in which more and more information is available to all stakeholders for multiple purposes.

- A number of countries in the LAC region have updated privacy protection legislation. However, the enormous gap between regulation and actual implementation of privacy standards in the region challenges individual constitutional rights. Legislation and regulation without the institutional capacity to implement it cannot be effective.

- While data manipulation can provide direct benefits to government agencies, companies and users, current policies and practice in the region with respect to data protection, surveillance, and privacy intrusion, are inadequate. Abuse is becoming increasingly common and people are increasingly subject to various forms of discrimination, often without being aware of it.

- Mechanisms for holding States accountable for the protection of their citizens' privacy must be strengthened and others are needed to evaluate private sector actors and ensure that their practices with respect to the collection and processing of information about citizens meet the standards expected of them. It is important to consider the sanctions available for use against those who infringe on privacy, whether they are being applied and whether they are effective.

Embedded in many of these proposals is a decisive call for more evidence to guide policy and for an ongoing dialogue among experts exploring these issues in the context of building more inclusive information societies. To enable policy makers and other stakeholders to make sense of developments in the information societies of Latin American and Caribbean countries with their many distinctive characteristics, it is important to monitor progress on several fronts. As a community representing different perspectives, we need to develop the evidence, to debate in-depth the implications of various policy options and actively respond to the emerging challenges and opportunities. The aim must be to discover which initiatives lead to success or to failure, and to ensure learning from the many diverse experiences of innovation in information societies in the region.

By investing in gathering evidence about developments in all these areas it will be possible to move beyond 'access' to consider many of the critical issues that will affect how people and their communities experience their information societies in the coming years. This does not mean abandoning work on the digital divide or on access and use of ICTs. But it does mean paying more attention to the emerging possibilities for users and citizens to learn, to be creative and to improve their lives, as well as to the obstacles that would reinforce inequality and restrict the inclusiveness of the emerging information society.

The need to address these themes in the agenda of Latin America and Caribbean countries is aligned with other global efforts towards more inclusive information societies. For instance, in the 'Renewing the Knowledge Societies Vision' report[3], the authors highlight that "It is essential to recall that knowledge societies are concerned with human development, not only with technological innovation and its impacts". Access to information and networks is a basic requirement for creating information societies, but not a sufficient requirement. Acquiring and applying knowledge implies understanding meaning and participation. Access to knowledge requires more than access to computers or mobile phones or even digital

---

[3]   Mansell, Robin and Tremblay, Gaëtan. 2013. *Renewing the knowledge societies vision: towards knowledge societies for peace and sustainable development.* WSIS+10 Conference. UNESCO. Paris, France.

information. It requires learning; and learning occurs through experience.

There is a growing need for a better understanding of the specific developments in the LAC region with respect not only to access, but also to citizenship, intellectual property rights, privacy, and online entrepreneurship. Developments in all these areas will continue to affect the "user experience" of information societies. Understanding them is essential if stakeholders in the region are to be able to understand how developments in their information societies are influencing culture, employment, health, political participation and the development of markets. The full potential of information societies will be achieved only if the balance between closed, open, and in-between strategies for information society development is understood.

Made in the USA
Charleston, SC
21 December 2013